THE
MONKEY
BUSINESS

NILES ELDREDGE is a curator in the Department of Invertebrates at The American Museum of Natural History in New York City. A paleontologist, Eldredge's specialty is trilobites, extinct relatives of crabs and shrimp. He has collected fossils extensively in North America, Europe and Egypt, and is currently studying 380-million-year-old trilobites from Bolivia, Brazil and South Africa.

In addition to trilobites, his main professional concern is to improve the connection between evolutionary theory and our knowledge of the fossil record. With Joel Cracraft, he is the author of *Phylogenetic Patterns and the Evolutionary Process* (1980) and, with Ian Tattersall, *The Myths of Human Evolution* (1982). Eldredge, his wife Michelle and their two sons, Douglas and Gregory, live in New Jersey and repair—not often enough—to the Adirondack Mountains to go fishing and hiking.

THE MONKEY BUSINESS

A Scientist Looks at Creationism

Niles Eldredge

WASHINGTON SQUARE PRESS
PUBLISHED BY POCKET BOOKS NEW YORK

An *Original* publication of WASHINGTON SQUARE PRESS

 A Washington Square Press Publication of
POCKET BOOKS, a Simon & Schuster division of
GULF & WESTERN CORPORATION
1230 Avenue of the Americas, New York, N.Y. 10020

ISBN: 0-671-44115-9

First Washington Square Press printing April, 1982

10 9 8 7 6 5 4 3 2 1

CONTENTS

PREFACE

"IN THE BEGINNING GOD CREATED THE HEAVEN AND the earth. And the earth was without form, and void; and darkness was upon the face of the deep. And the Spirit of God moved upon the face of the waters.

"And God said, Let there be light: and there was light. And God saw the light, that it was good: and God divided the light from the darkness. And God called the light Day, and the darkness he called Night. And the evening and the morning were the first day.

"And God said, Let there be a firmament in the midst of the waters, and let it divide the waters from the waters. And God made the firmament, and divided the waters which were under the firmament from the waters which were above the firmament: and it was so. And God called the firmament Heaven. And the evening and the morning were the second day.

"And God said, Let the waters under the heaven be gathered together unto one place, and let the dry land appear: and it was so. And God called the dry land Earth; and the gathering together of the waters called he Seas: and God saw that it was good. And God said, Let the earth bring forth grass, the herb yielding seed, and the fruit tree yielding fruit after his kind, whose seed is in itself, upon the earth: and it was so. And the earth brought forth grass, and herb yielding seed after his kind, and the tree yielding fruit, whose seed was in itself, after his kind: and God saw that it was good. And the evening and the morning were the third day.

"And God said, Let there be lights in the firmament of the heaven to divide the day from the night; and let them be for signs, and for seasons, and for days and years: And let them be for lights in the firmament of the heaven to give light upon the earth: and it was so. And God made two great lights; the greater light to rule the day, and the lesser light to rule the night: he made the stars also. And God set them in the firmament of the heaven to give light upon the earth, and to rule over the day and over the night, and to divide the light from the darkness: and God saw that it was good. And the evening and the morning were the fourth day.

"And God said, Let the waters bring forth abundantly the moving creature that hath life, and fowl that may fly above the earth in the open firmament of heaven. And God created great whales, and every living creature that moveth, which the waters brought forth abundantly, after their kind, and every winged fowl after his kind: and God saw that it was good. And God blessed them, saying, Be fruitful, and multiply, and fill the waters in the seas, and let fowl multiply in the earth. And the evening and the morning were the fifth day.

"And God said, Let the earth bring forth the living creature after his kind, cattle, and creeping thing, and beast of the earth after his kind: and it was so. And God made the beast of the earth after his kind, and cattle after their kind, and every thing that creepeth upon the earth after his kind: and God saw that it was good.

"And God said, Let us make man in our image, after our likeness: and let them have dominion over the fish of the sea, and over the fowl of the air, and over the cattle, and over all the earth, and over every creeping thing that creepeth upon the earth. So God created man in his own image, in the image of God created he him; male and female created he them. And God blessed them, and God said unto them, Be fruitful, and multiply, and replenish the earth, and subdue it: and have dominion over the fish of the sea, and over the fowl of the air, and over every living thing that moveth upon the earth. And God said, Behold, I have given you every herb bearing seed, which is upon the face of all the earth, and every tree, in which is the fruit of a tree yielding seed; to you it shall be for meat. And to every beast of the earth, and to every fowl of the air, and to every thing that creepeth upon the earth, wherein there is life, I have given every green herb for meat: and it was so. And God saw every thing that he had made, and, behold, it was very good. And the evening and the morning were the sixth day." (Genesis 1, King James Version)

Many words have been written about the origins of things, but none have been strung together quite so well as these of the first chapter of Genesis. A "biblical creationist" sees these words as having a literal truth spoken by God, and says, "These words are enough to explain all things." A "scientific creationist" respects these words as the literal truth, but seeks to prove the account in Genesis by scientific evidence, and by disproving evolution and attacking geology. Still, a "scientific creationist" would only ask for one change in the text: that instead of "God" we read "Creator" throughout Genesis.

These two sorts of creationists label a "theistic evolutionist" any person who reads Genesis metaphorically, who believes God created heaven and earth and all of life, but did so using His own natural laws. To such a person, the six days of creation square well with the eons of geologic time in a definite, albeit loose, sense.

A theistic evolutionist would leave the text alone, but does not insist that it be taken literally.

Lastly, we have the scientist who may have any conceivable personal opinion about Genesis, but who by the rules of his profession must consider the origin of all things natural solely in naturalistic terms. He must leave to religion all things supernatural.

The aim of this book is to look at the contemporary collisions between these various attitudes about Genesis—collisions that have lately caused quite a stir. It takes the position that religion and science are two utterly different domains of human experience, have little in common, and must respect each other if either is to flourish. As a scientist, I am repelled by the pseudoscience of the scientific creationists. And I have personally observed the passion and the anger some religious leaders have expressed when they confront "scientific creationism." It seems to me that the beauty and relevance of Genesis 1 are neither threatened nor enhanced by modern science. Why can't we just let it be and get on with the job of understanding ourselves and our world in our respective, time-honored ways?

THE
MONKEY
BUSINESS

Chapter 1

ONCE MORE UNTO THE BREACH . . . CREATIONISM REVISITED

MANY AMERICANS WERE STUNNED WHEN JUDGE IRVing Perluss of the Superior Court of California banged his gavel to open the proceedings the press had already dubbed "Scopes II." How could modern, sophisticated America have slipped back so far into the past? Memories of Clarence Darrow battling it out with William Jennings Bryan in the sultry, sweaty, summer days of 1925 in Dayton, Tennessee, came flooding back—though the press reserved most of the nostalgia for H. L. Mencken's trenchant trial coverage for the *Baltimore Sun*. Surely the enlightened forces of science had fully triumphed in Scopes "I." Surely all attempts to inject fundamentalist Christian interpretations of Genesis into public school curricula had been abandoned over half a century ago. What went wrong?

Nothing "went wrong." Though the United States today is more dependent upon technology and its scientific underpinnings than ever before, there is precious little evidence that we as a nation are any more sophisticated than we were in 1925. The myth that our tradition of technological advancement implies similar progress in all things blinds us to the simple historical fact that the United States has had an even richer tradi-

tion of anti-intellectualism. It is far more appropriate
to think of a pendulum of popularity in styles of
thought, belief, and action, than to invoke the imagery
of an unswerving arrow of progress when confronting
a phenomenon like the recent upsurge of creationism
in the United States.

The truth is that the original Scopes trial was far
more a victory for creationists than for their opponents.
John Scopes was, in fact, convicted of violating the
Tennessee statute known as the Butler Act, which said
in part:

> . . . it shall be unlawful for any teacher in any of
> the Universities, Normals and all other public
> schools of the State which are supported in whole
> or in part by the public school funds of the State,
> to teach any theory that denies the story of the
> Divine Creation of man as taught in the Bible,
> and to teach instead that man has descended from
> a lower order of animals.

Clarence Darrow and his colleagues, including a
battery of lawyers from the American Civil Liberties
Union, never disputed the charge that John Scopes had
indeed taught the evolution segment of the biology
curriculum. (It is an amusing sidelight that, later in
life, Scopes admitted he had in fact *never* taught evolution to his biology class—though he had covered the
subject in general science.) Convicted of his "crime,"
Scopes was fined $100.00. The Tennessee Supreme
Court then threw out the conviction on the technicality
that Judge Ralston had improperly levied the fine on
Scopes: Tennessee law mandated that only a jury could
impose fines of $50.00 or more. The action stymied
the plans of Darrow and colleagues: their real aim was
to have the law reviewed and thrown out by the U.S.
Supreme Court. Their argument, of course, was to be
that the law stood in violation of the Constitution, par-

ticularly the establishment clause of the First Amendment prohibiting the mixing of church and state.

The issue of creationism in the classroom finally reached the U.S. Supreme Court in 1968 in *Epperson* v. *Arkansas*. Mrs. Epperson, a Little Rock high school biology teacher, successfully challenged a 1929 Arkansas law forbidding the teaching of "the theory or doctrine that mankind ascended or descended from a lower order of animals." Not until the Supreme Court ruled that the Arkansas law was "an attempt to blot out a particular theory because of its supposed conflict with the Biblical account," and thus an attempt to establish religion in the classroom, was the Tennessee and other similar statutes declared null and void.

Certainly not legally dead as a result of the Scopes trial, creationism maintained a steady though low profile through the next fifty years. And the most subtle yet profound sign that the creationists had won in an important sense in 1925 was the dramatic downplay evolution received in high school biology texts from the late 1920s until comparatively recently. George W. Hunter's *Civic Biology*, published in 1914—the book Scopes testified he used in his course—originally had a brief discussion of evolution. After the trial, the publishers brought out a revised edition *(New Civic Biology)* eliminating any mention of evolution. Virtually all other texts followed suit. If Genesis had not quite made it into the classroom, the Scopes trial did place a tremendous damper on the teaching of evolution for the next thirty-five years or so. Only when Americans awoke to see Sputnik circling the earth—and awoke thereby to the woeful inadequacies of science education in the United States—was anything done. The resulting massive, national effort to upgrade the quality of science education included evolution—in a sense priming the pump for the battles now underway in virtually every state of the union.

No, creationism never did go away. It merely receded through the Depression and World War II, with their massive public programs. It also remained largely dormant in the fat, complacent 1950s, too, and few of us heard much about it in the radical, activist 1960s—though it was then that Mrs. Epperson was able to mount a successful challenge to the monkey laws still on the books. Why, then, is it such a popular issue now?

Creationism—the belief that the cosmos, the earth, and all of life are the separate acts of a supernatural Creator—is most closely associated in the United States with various sects of fundamentalist Christianity. Other religions (for instance, some Orthodox Jewish sects) also reject the scientific notion of evolution in favor of a literal biblical rendition of the origins of the earth and living things. Indeed, the religions of nearly all known societies have creation myths that explain the origin of the world, who people are, how they came to be, and why.

But creationism is far more than a religious belief. As fascinating as the comparative study of creation stories may be, it is the political nature of creationism in the United States that gave the topic its importance in 1925, as it has once again today. William Jennings Bryan, the sterling symbol of grass-roots populism who ran for the presidency three times and once served as Secretary of State, was the spokesman for fundamentalist beliefs against the supposedly godless forces of evolution in the Scopes trial. Long past his prime as an orator (he died only three days after the trial ended), Bryan nonetheless stirred the hearts of creationists during the trial, with his masterful blend of religion and politics. No one (except journalist H. L. Mencken) objected to the right of a student to believe whatever he or she wanted. But the activist side of creationism, which attempts to see religious-inspired belief taught in schools (or evolution expunged from the curriculum), leaves the arena of religion and enters the world of politics.

The current rise of creationism can only be under-

stood as a part of the general upsurge of "neopopu-
lism." The new conservatism sweeping America—a
conservatism as much anti-General Motors as it is
anti-United Auto Workers—opposes big companies,
big unions, and big government. It seeks more local
control of tax dollars and the programs those dollars
support. The tax revolt and the attack on a host of
issues (e.g., sex education, abortion, the Equal Rights
Amendment) are all designed to support what are
perceived as traditional American family values. The
Moral Majority, which is pro creationist and anti-
evolutionist, is merely the latest, most visible, and most
successful religious organization (primarily fundamentalist Protestant) to engage in overt political action. The
populist form of conservative politics has always gone
hand in hand with conservative Protestant religious belief. Small wonder creationism is once more on the
political scene.

Thus, the central importance of creationism today is
its political nature. Creationists travel all over the
United States, visiting college campuses and staging
"debates" with biologists, geologists, and anthropologists. The creationists nearly always win. The audience
is frequently loaded with the already converted and the
faithful. And scientists, until recently, have been showing up at the debates ill-prepared for what awaits them.
Thinking the creationists are uneducated, Bible-thump-
ing clods, they are soon routed by a steady onslaught
of direct attacks on a wide variety of scientific topics.
No scientist has an expert's grasp of all the relevant
points of astronomy, physics, chemistry, biology, geology, and anthropology. Creationists today—at least the
majority of their spokesmen—are highly educated, in-
telligent people. Skilled debaters, they have always done
their homework. And they nearly always seem better
informed than their opponents, who are reduced too
often to a bewildered state of incoherence. As will be
all too evident when we examine the creationist position in detail, their arguments are devoid of any real

intellectual content. Creationists win debates because of their canny stage presence, and not through clarity of logic or force of evidence. The debates are shows rather than serious considerations of evolution.

The debate tactic reveals the essence of the creationist approach: the collision between creation and evolution is still presented as an unresolved, intellectual problem. When Darwin published the *Origin of Species* in 1859, he sparked a genuine controversy. Did a naturalistic explanation of the origin and development of life on earth pose a serious *theological* challenge? Thomas Henry Huxley (Aldous' and Julian's grandfather and Darwin's main champion in England) debated Bishop Wilberforce soon after the *Origin* appeared. But such theological problems as evolution seemed to pose were soon resolved; most Christian and Jewish thinkers today see no conflict between science and religion. Science seeks to understand the universe in naturalistic terms. It depends upon observation, accepts nothing on faith, and acknowledges that it can never claim to know the ultimate truth. Religions, on the other hand, are belief systems, generally involving the supernatural. Both are time-honored—but utterly different—human activities. Most scientists and members of religious communities see no conflict, as the two systems are completely different, are pursued for different reasons, and serve different functions.

Fundamentalism is literally the belief in a list of five essential ("fundamental") points of Christianity as put forth by the Niagara Bible Conference in 1895: the inerrancy of the Bible, the divinity of Jesus, his virgin birth, the atonement of mankind's sins by his crucifixion, and his resurrection and eventual Second Coming. Thus for some sects there is, on the face of it, still a collision between science and religion. Though the debate for the most part has left purely theological circles, it *is* the perception of fundamentalists that science and religion are in conflict that underlies the creationist endeavor.

Hence the form of the college debates. Creationists don't argue religion. Far from it. Their tactic these days (to avoid First and Fourteenth Amendment charges) is to talk of "scientific creationism." The issue is still cast in purely intellectual terms: the biblical version (there are actually two in Genesis) of the origin of the earth, life, and mankind is recast in terms that seem scientific. An early example is Archbishop Ussher of Ireland, who in 1654, analyzing all the "begats" in Genesis and combining his results with other biblical hints, concluded that the earth was created on October 26, 4004 B.C. at 9:00 in the morning. Later biblical exegetes emended the date somewhat. But the basic result of such biblical scholarship is clear: if Genesis is literally correct, the earth is no more than a few thousand years old.

Nuclear physics, through its theories of atomic structure and radioactivity, has provided us with a means of actually calculating the age of formation of a rock. The process of radioactive decay is constant (a fact creationists challenge, by the way, but which nonetheless has withstood critical scrutiny in the laboratory). If we know the rate one elemental form (isotope) changes to another by radioactive decay, we can measure the amount of "parent" and "daughter" isotopes in the rock and come up with an estimate of how long ago the rock was formed. The oldest rocks yet dated on earth are granites from Greenland, approximately 3.8 billion years old. Because the oldest moon samples and all meteorites *always* yield dates of about 4.5 billion years, and because it is clear that the oldest rocks on earth have since been destroyed, geologists estimate the age of the formation of the earth at about 4.5 billion years ago.

Creationists have attacked the theory and practice of radiometric dating. And, as we shall see in Chapter 5, they have assembled a number of arguments based on supposed scientific data to support their claim that the earth is but a few thousand years old. This issue—

the age of the earth—is but one of many areas of contemporary science attacked by creationists, ostensibly on scientific grounds, but in reality only because their reading of Genesis and their belief in the infallibility of the Bible seem to them to require that conventional science must be wrong. Scientific creationism, with its basic assumption of a supernatural Creator, is a sectarian religious belief with a thin veneer of "science." Careful examination easily reveals that "scientific creationism" is not intellectually worthwhile science. *All* of the arguments and evidences adduced by creationists in their attempts to salvage a literal Genesis version of "creation" are outmoded, false, and (in some cases) downright dishonest distortions. The issue of creationism is not an intellectual problem on the scientific side any more than it is an intellectual issue on the theological side, that is, except to a few sects. We will take a closer look at the main tenets of scientific creationism in later chapters.

If the confrontation between creationism and science is not an intellectual problem, what is it? It is a social and political problem—and, specifically, an educational problem. The structure of the modern creationist argument goes like this: there are two competing theories (or "models," as creationists like to call them) that explain how the earth, life, and mankind all came to be as we see them today. One is the notion of evolution—basically, that the universe, with all its parts, was formed by natural processes in a gradual manner requiring millions and billions of years. The other—creationism—as we have already seen, views the origins as the separate acts of a supernatural Creator who a very short time ago, using laws no longer operative today, created what we now see out of nothing. Each such creation was a separate act, and such creation is no longer occurring.

Creationists argue that these two "models" are competing but totally comparable systems of belief. They are both authoritarian belief systems. Creationists are constantly asking the question: Which would you prefer your children to *believe*—evolution or creation? At this point, the creationist strategy diverges. Depending upon the intended audience and the preference of the particular individual, a creationist will argue that evolution and creationism are comparable belief systems either because (1) both are scientific, or (2) both are actually forms of religious belief. Creationists have been very successful of late in converting student followers, having favorable rulings adopted by local school boards, and even getting legislation passed in state legislatures precisely through this ploy. By claiming the two models are equally viable, they appeal to the traditional American sense of "fair play" to include *both* in the school curriculum. Why not let the students decide which is the more convincing?

Equating creationism with evolution lies at the heart of the creationist movement in the 1980s. In the following chapters we will examine the basis for this assertion in detail. We will see what science is, and that evolution is most definitely "scientific." And we will look at creationist claims that evolution is really a religion, as well as their more usual cry that creationism is truly scientific. To the extent that creationism is science, of course, it is merely bad science. Mostly, it isn't science at all.

If the "intellectual" content of the controversy is virtually nil, a mere ploy to give a veneer of credibility to an otherwise blatantly religiously inspired political activity, why concern ourselves at all with this issue? The science reporter for one of the major television networks asked me recently if it really mattered what some students in some states were taught about evolution. Who cares?

My concern is not that every student in the United States should learn the ABC's of evolution, of what science thinks happened during the long history of life and how new forms of animal and plant life spring

from old. But since this country, for better or worse,
is locked into a technology-dependent future, *there is
no alternative*. Much as many of us (neopopulists or
not) would love to return to the halcyon days of a
simpler time (though much of this desire is clearly
fantasy anyway), we would all soon starve. Going back
to an economic system less directly dependent on high
technology (and the science that underlies it) is simply
impossible. We have made our bed. The best way to lie
in it is to maintain the very highest standards of science
education in the United States. School children should
be taught not so much what science currently thinks
about why roses are red and violets blue, but rather
who scientists are and how they operate. What *is*
science, anyway?

Creationism seeks to dilute the science curriculum
with the equivalent of medical quackery. It seeks to
delude our kids into believing that scientists are so
dumb that they have been misled by the Creator's mis-
chievous attempts to deceive us: if the earth is really
only 10,000 years old, why did the Creator create an
earth with so many hints that it really is vastly older?
Kids don't need to "believe" evolution—but surely they
ought to know that all reputable biological scientists
see evolution as the *only* naturalistic, scientific explanation of the order we see in the biological side of nature.
They ought to know that, in principle, the notion of
evolution is *falsifiable*—we can, theoretically, throw it
out should the evidence one day point that way. This
is how knowledge is accumulated. Learning from our
mistakes, we get closer to the truth only when we realize that what we once *thought* was right is really wrong.
Creationists tenaciously cling to the wisdom and world
view of a Near Eastern culture thousands of years old.
According to creationists, nothing in the Bible could
possibly be wrong. The doubt and uncertainty, the need
to make progress by showing older ideas to be wrong—
which is the backbone of scientific inquiry—is simply

alien and unacceptable to creationists. Students ought
to know that the evidence for evolution has been
scrupulously scrutinized daily by thousands of biologists for well over a hundred years—and no one yet
has called a press conference trumpeting his new proof
that evolution has *not* occurred. Evolution is as well-
established a scientific notion as gravity. A student
ought to know that.

So creationism seems to me to threaten the integrity
of our children's education, and thus threaten the
long-term well-being of our country. It is a pseudo-
intellectual collision between science and (a certain
brand of) religion, politicized and fought over in legislatures, courtrooms, and at school-board meetings. Professional creationists (we'll be taking a look at the
activities of a number of creationist organizations currently active in the United States) in San Diego draft
model legislation and motions adopted by state legislatures and local school boards in Arkansas and Atlanta.
Professional scientists join the fray, parading fossil
horses on magazine-format television shows to counter
the creationist claim that there is no evidence directly
in favor of evolution.

All of this is highly visible, and has recently grabbed
a great deal of media space. But it is in the classroom
that the real battle is being fought, and, I fear, largely
lost these days. Parental and local political and religious pressure on teachers is often severe—in the North
as well as the South, in Scarsdale, New York, as much
as in San Diego, California. Teachers in the trenches
derive small comfort from the Olympian pronouncements of professional scientists—it is they, the teachers,
who must come up with quick answers when asked
why they don't teach the "dual model" approach. Creationists are actively lobbying *locally*, making presentations ridiculing evolution, citing prominent scientists
(out of context, of course) to the effect that the fossil
record flatly falsifies the very notion of evolution. At
the local level, all manner of distortion and trickery is

made use of—there is only the merest pretense of accuracy. There, the gloves are off. The only response must be a concerted counterattack on the local level: support for the beleaguered school systems by well-informed, concerned citizens who care about the future of American education.

Chapter 2

AMERICA AND SCIENCE:
HAM AND EGGS OR CATS AND DOGS?

THOSE OF US WITH SMALL CHILDREN ARE ALL TOO FA-
miliar with the endless parade of Saturday morning
cartoon shows. The forces of good are constantly pitted
against the seemingly superior strength of malevolence.
The good guys—usually teenagers—win with a combination of American smarts and a bit of luck.

The bad guys are despots, privy to some fanciful,
advanced, and dangerous technology. Or they are
simply mad scientists. The message is strikingly clear:
at best scientists know nothing of the social implications of their work; at worst, they want power. They
want to build modern-day versions of Frankenstein's
monster and take over the world.

On the other hand, Americans read fad-diet books,
take pride in the Space Shuttle, and rush to buy the
latest electric gadget for the kitchen. Americans are
more pleased with their video-cassette recorders than
they are displeased with toxic waste sites. By and large,
this is a reasonable view: both the blessings and the
ills spawned by technology come from "science." But
so dedicated are we to the medical and other technological signs of progress that, in this quarter, science wins.
The scientists in the labs are wizards who prolong our

lives, make them more comfortable, and keep America safe for democracy.

White hats/black hats. America has a thoroughly ambivalent view of scientists. But perhaps the two attitudes are not all that far apart, after all. Both seem to be based on the notion that scientists are a special class of people—removed from the typical daily concerns of ordinary people. Scientists are said to have a special way of thinking—the "scientific method"—that sets them apart from the rest of society. If the isolation and deep thought sometimes lead to madness, they also encourage the wizardry that improves the whiteness factor in laundry detergents and puts computers at the checkout stations in supermarkets.

It is the scientific method that sets scientists apart, for better or worse, for good or evil, from the rest of society. One of the most misunderstood—and thereby overrated—procedures yet devised, the scientific method is supposed to lead to the "truth" about things by the combination of meticulous, repeated observation, experimentation, and careful thought, tinged with occasional flashes of rare insight, the "Eureka!"s of the truly innovative scientific mind.

By perpetuating the myth that they are privy to some form of higher mental processes, scientists have made a big mistake in simple public relations. How can the public think otherwise if most scientists themselves believe that their techniques and procedures, their scientific method, set them apart from all others? Many scientists really do seem to believe they have a special access to the truth. They call press conferences to trumpet marvelous new discoveries. They compete hard for awards and prizes. And they expect to be believed—by their peers and, especially, by the public at large. Throwing down scientific thunderbolts from Olympian heights, scientists come across as authoritarian truthgivers whose word must be taken unquestioned. That all the evidence shows the behavior of scientists clearly to be no different from the ways in which other people behave is somehow overlooked in all this.

The creationists have seen this self-important side of science and have exploited it to the hilt. Noting that evolutionary biologists still tend to react to creationists by asserting that *they* know the truth, creationist lawyer Richard K. Turner remarked after the 1981 "Scopes II" trial in California: "These scientists get up on the stand, and act as if their very lives were being attacked. They not only close ranks, but they almost deny anybody the right to know of the internal fights that go on within the evolutionary crowd. They're pompous and arrogant, just the kind of people that the First Amendment was written to protect us against." Until comparatively recently, scientists have responded to creationist challenges simply by asserting: *We* are the scientists, believe *us*. And the creationists have exploited this situation very cleverly: if scientists are willing to compete for people's belief, the creationists can then argue that the traditional sense of American fair play should hold. Standard scientific thought in the last quarter of the twentieth century comes across as just another authoritarian belief system. That being the case, creationists argue that it is only right and proper that the children in school should hear about the particular alternative belief system the creationists want to push.

But, of course, science is *not* a belief system. Science is the human search for a natural explanation of what the universe is: how it is constructed, how it came to be. The only rule of the scientific method is that we must discard any scientific statement if the evidence of our senses shows it is wrong. To be scientific, we must be able to go to Mother Nature to see if an idea works, to see if it fits. If we cannot go out and test the validity of a notion directly, we can take a more circuitous route: if an explanation about the world is correct, it must imply some further consequences that we can observe in nature. If we fail to find these predicted consequences, if instead we observe something else, then our explanation can't be correct. If we *do* make the predicted observations, temporarily the explanation has defied our attempts to show it is false.

And that is the simple essence of science. No idea is sacred. No statement is the ultimate truth. It is in the very nature of things that precious few ideas put forth to date in science have entirely withstood the test of time. Evolution is one. So is the idea that the earth is round.

Facts and Theories: Is the Earth Really Round?

When Ronald Reagan injected creationism into the 1980 presidential campaign, he took a familiar route. Referring to evolution, he told reporters (after speaking to a group of fundamentalists in Dallas, Texas): "Well, it is a theory, a scientific theory only, and it has in recent years been challenged in the world of science and is not yet believed in the scientific community to be as infallible as it once was believed."

Beyond the fascinating commingling of politics, religion, and science, Reagan's remark picked up a standard creationist ploy when he said that evolution is "a theory, a scientific theory only." And it is true that most of us use the word "theory" to mean some tentative, sketchy notion about why or how something happened. All of us, for instance, have our own "theory" on how and why Reagan was elected, why the oil companies really have been raising prices, and why inflation has been so bad in recent years. This is standard usage. But creationists, including some who claim *bona fide* scientific credentials, have exploited the vernacular connotation of the word "theory," in effect saying that scientists use "theory" in precisely the same way. Thus, if evolution is only a theory, our confidence in it ought to be less than if it were, say, a "fact." "Theories" turn into "hare-brained ideas" with ease. "Theory" is a bad

word: to call an idea a theory is to impugn its credibility.

But theories in science are merely ideas: a theory
may be a single, simple idea or, more usually, a complex set of ideas. Some are good and have withstood
the test of time well. Evolution—specifically, the notion
that all organisms past and present are interrelated by
a process of ancestry and descent—is such a theory.
On the other hand, some theories have stood the test
of time poorly and are no longer credited with much
explanatory power. Spontaneous generation—the idea
that organisms sprang from inorganic beginnings *de
novo*, and are not all interrelated—has long been dis-
carded as a useful scientific notion. It is taught in
schools today, if at all, only as a historical curiosity.

Philosophers of science have argued long and hard
over the differences between facts, hypotheses, and
theories. But the real point is this: they are all essentially the same. All of them are ideas. Some ideas are
more credible than others. If the overwhelming evidence of our senses suggests some idea is correct, we
call it a fact. But the fact remains that a "fact" is an
idea.

Consider the statement, "The earth is round." Is it a
fact, an hypothesis, or a theory? A prominent creationist I once spoke to took offense at my suggestion that
dismissing evolution as a credible notion was no different in principle from denying that the earth is round.
To him, and to most of us, that the earth is round is
a fact. But why? How many of us can perform a critical
experiment to show that the earth really is round? How
many of us have ventured high enough into the upper
reaches of the earth's atmosphere that we could really
see the earth's curvature? Most of us have seen photos
of the earth taken from satellites, space ships, and
from the moon itself. Clearly the earth is round. But
the relatively few vocal "flat earthers" have a counter
even for this: the spectacular achievements in space of
the past twenty-five years are all an elaborate hoax—

nothing more. The stills and film of a round earth are fakes.

Now, *if* the earth is round, it is probably safe to assume it has always been so—at least since the dawn of human history when we can pick up a written record of mankind's views on the question. Yet the roundness of the earth was certainly no generally accepted fact when Columbus set sail with his fleet of three ships. Only after the globe had been safely circumnavigated a number of times without a single ship dropping off the edge did the roundness of the earth start to take on the dimensions of credibility we deem necessary for a notion to become a fact.

Yet Eratosthenes, a Greek living in Ptolemaic Egypt in the third century B.C., showed that the earth could not be flat with a simple yet conclusive experiment. His predecessors had already suggested the earth was round because it cast a curved shadow on the moon. And ships sailing toward an observer appeared on the horizon from the top of the mast down, also suggesting the earth is curved. Hearing that the sun shone directly down a well at Syene (now Aswan) at noon on the summer solstice (the longest day of the year), Eratosthenes measured the angle between the sun's rays and a plumb bob he lowered down a well in Alexandria, some six hundred miles north of Aswan, precisely at noon. That there was an angle at all in Alexandria was inconsistent with the idea that the earth was flat. The phenomenon could only be explained if he envisaged a ball-shaped earth. Using simple trigonometry, Eratosthenes calculated the circumference of the earth to be the equivalent of about 28,000 miles, a respectable approximation to the 24,857 miles our modern instruments give us today. Columbus was aware of this and of later calculations, and used them in his navigation.

Certainly the universe is the way it is notwithstanding what we may *think* it is. Is the proposition that the earth is round a fact, an hypothesis, a theory, or a downright falsehood? It is an idea that has been variously considered all four. It was first called a wild idea, then a necessary conclusion (albeit accepted only by a few Greek savants); its respectability as a credible idea grew with the Renaissance. Now most of us proclaim it as fact—all attempts to disprove it have utterly failed. Flat earthers notwithstanding, we now even have direct confirmatory photographic evidence that the earth is a sphere. But a round earth is still an idea, albeit an extraordinarily powerful idea.

So what of Ronald Reagan's remark that evolution is *only* a theory? The answer is this: *all* of science is an interplay of ideas and observations. To label something a theory in science is really to call it a complex idea. And that is what science is all about: ideas.

Evolution: How Good an Idea Is It?

Evolution is the idea that all of the ten million or so species of organisms on earth today have descended from a single common ancestor. The much misused expression "evolutionary theory" refers to two rather different sorts of things. When biologists speak of "evolutionary theory," they are referring to ideas about *how* the evolutionary process actually works: How do new species arise from old ones? How were four toes reduced to but a single digit on the front feet of horses during the course of their fifty-million-year history?

On the other hand, creationists (and the public at large) understand the expression "evolutionary theory," or "the theory of evolution" to mean "the proposition that life has evolved." Here scientists, understandably, get upset. "Evolution is a fact," they say. And, in the sense that the "theory of evolution" means "life has evolved," it is true that all attempts to show that all organisms are *not* interrelated (in other words, all attempts to falsify the very idea of evolution) have failed as egregiously as have attempts to show that the earth is not round. Evolution is a fact as much as the idea that the earth is shaped like a ball. But both facts remain ideas—falsifiable, scientific ideas.

On the other hand, flat assertions that evolution is a fact have actually boomeranged, as the public sees such pronouncements simply as part of a shouting match: rather like the old joke about the difference between Northern and Southern Baptists (Northerner: There ain't no hell. Southerner: The hell there ain't!). Scientists say evolution has occurred, creationists say it hasn't. Which side is the public to believe?

To repeat, science is not a belief system. Evolution is the only scientific notion still left in biology that explains the mountain of information about life past and present that has been amassed over the past two hundred years or so. All other ideas (such as spontaneous generation) have bitten the scientific dust. The basic idea that life has evolved explains how the face of the organic world has come to be as we see it today and does so without recourse to supernatural beings or special rules. It says that the simple process of ancestry and descent, as purely a natural process as parental ancestry and descent among human beings, is responsible for the order, the beautiful pattern of similarity interlinking all forms of life. Evolution is "descent with modification"—to use the phrase of Charles Darwin himself. The descent links up all forms of life. The modification leads to diversification: today we have radishes, owls, ourselves, and a good deal more; we are not all single-celled algae lying at the bottom of the ocean. Yet all forms of life are united by fundamental chemical and anatomical similarities.

Is evolution a scientific notion, and if so, how good is it? We will explore the other meaning of evolutionary theory (i.e., *how* life evolves) from this point of view in a later chapter. But now we ask: How good a scientific notion is the simple idea that life has evolved?

Creationists are fond of pointing to the obvious fact that events that happened in the past are not subject to experimental verification or falsification, or to direct observation. How can we study something that has already happened? And creationists also note that few reputable biologists seem willing to predict what will happen next in evolution. After all, if evolution is a scientific theory, it must be predictive. Scientists cannot or will not· predict the evolutionary future—strong evidence, indeed, that the very idea of evolution isn't scientific at all, according to this creationist interpretation of science.

All this fancy rhetoric beclouds the simple meaning of "predictivity" in science. As we have seen, predictivity means that *if* an idea is true, there should be certain consequences. We should be able to go to nature to see if these expected (predicted) consequences seem to be there. In this spirit, we simply ask: If the basic idea is correct that all organisms past and present are interrelated by a process of ancestry and descent we call evolution, what should we expect to find in the real world as a consequence? These observable consequences are the predictions we should be making—not guesses about the future. And one prediction would surely be that life has had a history—a long, intricate history of the very sort creationists deny. The fundamental prediction that there is a natural, coherent history of life is a strength of the very idea of evolution, not a fundamental stumbling block because of the problems faced by all historians, including those who examine human history as well as those who study the history of the universe, the earth and all of life.

So, evolution predicts that life has had a single, if long and complicated, history. As we shall see, the fossil record of life is some 3.5 billion years long, and the geologic sequence over the eons records hundreds of thousands of major vicissitudes in the long history of life. Creationists are forced to deny the earth is older than a few tens of thousands of years: the simple existence of such an old earth with such an immensely long and kaleidoscopically changing sequence of fossils immediately negates the creationist position and is a prediction consistent with the basic idea that life has evolved. Were the earth not so old, were there not any manifest *history* to life over truly long periods of time, the very idea of evolution would itself be suspect. Small wonder creationists devote so much time to denying that the earth is old and that the fossil record represents over three billion years of life's varied existence on earth.

But we can do better than this. We can sharpen our predictions to the point where a fossil record isn't even necessary to test the fundamental notion that all forms of life have descended from a common ancestor. What should *modern* life look like if the basic idea of evolution is correct? What predictions would we make?

Consider, as an analogy, the work of patient monks in the Middle Ages who laboriously copied manuscripts from remote times and thus saved us from knowing even less than we do about our ancient past. From time to time a monk would make a minor mistake as he copied—a happy circumstance, it turns out, for historians whose job it is to track down the development of modern versions of ancient texts. For each undetected mistake was faithfully copied by later generations. Here we have descent, but with modification: an early manuscript, free of errors, resembles its descendants to varying degrees. An error introduced into a copy is passed on to all subsequent copies. The result: the subsequent copies of manuscripts share more novelties (newly introduced items of change) than their earlier models do. If the copying in general has been accurate, all manuscripts will be fundamentally the same. But the *differences* between the manuscripts will be arranged so that later manuscripts will have more of the same changes in them than they will have in common with earlier manuscripts.

Now, consider the possibility that two monks copy the same manuscript, and each introduces a different mistake. Each of the new manuscripts is then copied by later monks. We now have two separate "lineages" of manuscripts. In each lineage, all manuscripts have something in common, while each succeeding manuscript has, in addition, more in common with its descendants than with the "ancestor." Both lineages converge at the "ancestral" manuscript and the two lineages share all those features of the original that have not been modified by errors in copying over the ensuing centuries. This analogy (though now rendered obsolete by photocopy machines) is apt: professionals make this prediction and thus are able to study the history of manuscript transmission through the ages.

Now, if life has evolved, it must be true that each of the ten million or so species has had a history. We see that roses, say, are vastly different from ourselves—thus the two-monks-copying-one-manuscript analogy must be in force. In other words, if life has evolved, it has also diversified. We don't find just one final form of life (or one final manuscript), but a whole host of different forms of life. What, then, does the notion of evolution predict about life?

If all of life, all of the ten million diverse species we see around us today, has descended from a single common ancestor, then there *must* be some fundamental similarities shared by all living things. We would predict that, simply because not all of the features of an ancestral life form would be modified so much that all traces of original, common ancestry would be lost. We would then predict that, as new species arose from old, changes in the genetic, anatomical, and behavioral properties would from time to time appear—just as the monks occasionally made mistakes in their copying. Later descendants would inherit these changes, while ancestors (whether survivors to the present, or found as fossils) would lack these features. And the very process of forming new species from old (where a new species buds off from a parental species) implies diversification: two species where once there was but one, or two monks copying the same original manuscript.

So, if the very idea of evolution is correct, there must be one coherent pattern of similarity interlinking *all* forms of life. For each separate species there is another also alive today to which it is more closely related than either are to any other living species. We can identify these close relatives because they share more properties with each other—more of the novelties produced within their own evolutionary branch—than they have in common with other organisms.

Here is another way of putting the prediction: the very idea of evolution implies that each species will tend to have some features unique to itself, but each species *must* share some similarities in structure or behavior with some other species. Furthermore, each group of similar species will share further features with other groups of species (the two-monk analogy again), and this common group *must* share features with still other groups. This pattern of sharing similarities with an ever-widening array of biological forms *must* continue until all of life is linked up by sharing at least one similarity in common. *This* is evolution's grand prediction: that the patterns of similarities in the organic world are arranged like a complex set of nested Chinese boxes.

Thus we can go to nature and easily test the basic notion of evolution. Does it work? Take any species and follow it out: dogs, say. Creationists are fond of dogs, saying, "Well, yes, perhaps coyotes and domestic dogs arose from wolves [as variants within 'basic kinds']—but there is no evidence that evolution has produced this group of doglike animals from any other 'major kind' [such as bears, cats, or weasels]." But if the fundamental notion of evolution is correct, there *must* be further resemblances between coyotes, wolves, and domestic dogs, on the one hand, and some other groups of animals. And, of course, there are: dogs are united with foxes and some extinct forms known only from fossils, because all share some peculiar features of the middle ear. This group (zoologists call them the

Family Canidae) share other similarities (particularly of the ear region) with bears, raccoons, and weasels. In turn, all these creatures share carnassial teeth (where the last upper premolar and first lower molar are bladelike and shear past each other like a pair of scissors) with cats, civets and seals: the group zoologists call the Order Carnivora. Carnivora, it turns out, share three middle-ear bones, mammary glands, placental development, hair, and a host of other features with a number of other organisms, including ourselves. These we call mammals. And so on. Mammals share with birds, lizards, snakes, and turtles an amniote egg, with its protective, enveloping tissues. Amniote animals share the property of having four legs with frogs and salamanders.

The kinship of dogdom widens as we see that some creatures, including all dogs, carnivores, mammals, and tetrapods, share backbones and other features with various sorts of animals we call fish. These, collectively, are the vertebrates. The circle widens to embrace progressively more groups: dogs, fungi, rosebushes, and amoebas have fundamentally similar (eukaryotic) cells. The eukaryotes are a massive, basic division of life—but they don't include bacteria and certain kinds of algae, for these are simpler yet, lacking the complex structures of the true eukaryotic cell. But bacteria and blue-green algae fall neatly into the fold when we look at the basic chemical constituents of cells. RNA (ribonucleic acid), which copies the structure of the genetic material (DNA) and sees that information translated into proteins, is found in all living things.

We started with dogs. We could have started with cats. The results would have quickly turned out to be the same (dogs and cats both being so closely related). Had we started with ourselves, *Homo sapiens* ("man the wise"), we would have found a pattern of ever-widening similarities, starting with the great apes, then ourselves + apes + old-world monkeys, then *that* group

(Anthropoidea) + new-world monkeys. Adding the lemurs and other "prosimians," we would have found what zoologists call the Order Primates. From then on, the branch quickly melds with the dog line: primates, like carnivores, are mammals; mammals are amniotes, etc.

Had we started with roses, the example would have taken longer to become the same: roses share properties with various berries (Family Rosaceae), which further share properties with other plants. All flowering plants are united by virtue of their shared mode of reproduction. All plants photosynthesize. Roses meet dogs only at the level of the Eukaryota. But the point is, they *do* meet.

Thus the basic prediction of evolution is confirmed: life, *all* life, as diverse as it is, is linked up in a hierarchical arrangement of similarities. This *must* be so if evolution has occurred. This, indeed, is what we find. But this is not the most important point. It is more important to see that the basic notion of evolution does have fundamental consequences that must be true if the very idea is correct. If we had failed to find this nested pattern of similarities interlinking all forms of life in our backyards, we would, as scientists, be forced by the rules of the game to reject the very notion of evolution. Evolution *is* predictive, and therefore thoroughly scientific.

On the other hand, the basic prediction of evolution, as we have just seen, is abundantly confirmed. Does this mean that we have proven evolution to be "true"? It is more accurate to say that, thus far, we have failed to *falsify* the notion of evolution, but it is always possible that new observations will show that the apparent pattern of progressive similarity that seems to link up all of life is, in some sense, false. Also, it is possible that someone in the future will come up with an idea other than evolution that will also predict the patterns of similarity we see in the organic realm.

As of this writing, no one has come up with an alternative, *testable* idea (one that yields predictions) to explain the patterns we all see. Creationists, of course, agree that there is a pattern of similarity connecting all forms of life. They merely claim that it pleased the Creator to fashion life in this way. But the Creator obviously could have fashioned each species in any way imaginable. There is no basis for us to make predictions about what we should find when we study animals and plants if we accept the basic creationist position.

Consider a more detailed way predictions are made in biology: We predict that, if we study some aspect of an organism—say, digestive enzymes or the fine internal structure of its teeth—we will find exactly the same pattern of similarities already seen between this organism and others when biologists before us examined the hair, skulls, and fingernails. We predict that patterns of similarity of as yet unexamined properties will agree with patterns already seen in more readily observable features. This must be so, if evolution is a viable notion, because life has had one single, coherent history. Creationists, on the other hand, cannot make such a prediction: the Creator could have fashioned each organ system or physiological process (such as digestion) in whatever fashion the Creator pleased.

This special notion of predictivity is vital to biomedical and agricultural research, which are the better-known areas of applied comparative biology. The news recently carried a report entirely typical of the logic and structure of this kind of research. A doctor in Tennessee found that thiamine (one of the "B" vitamins) has a great positive effect in the treatment of lead poisoning. He performed his initial experiments on calves. Switching over to rats, he was disappointed to find the results weaker and less dramatic. Obviously, he told his interviewer, we should try thiamine on monkeys and apes suffering from lead poisoning. Why would he want to do that?

The good doctor was predicting that our own physiology (after all, it is treatment of lead poisoning in humans that motivated the research) would be more similar to the physiologies of monkeys and apes, than to those of calves or rats. (Though because we share a more recent common ancestry with rats than with cows, I would predict that unfortunately his results with rats have greater implications for the treatment of lead poisoning in humans than do his results with calves.) Patterns of similarity seen in previous experience lead us to predict the existence of other, as yet unexamined, similarities. We expect the use of thiamine as a treatment for lead poisoning in humans to be more similar to its effects on monkeys and apes than on either calves or rats, simply because we have known for centuries that we share more features with apes and monkeys than we share with any other sort of creature. It is this predictive feature of evolution, then, that underlies the entire rationale of biomedical experimentation on animals other than ourselves to assess the value and safety of various compounds to alleviate human ailments.

This simple prediction—that there is one grand pattern of similarity linking up all life—doesn't *prove* evolution. But the failure of scientists to *disprove* evolution over the past two hundred years of comparative biological research means that evolution really is one of the few grand ideas of biology that has stood the test of time. The basic notion of evolution is thoroughly scientific in the strictest sense of the word, and as such is as highly corroborated and at least as powerful as the notion of gravity or the idea that the earth is round, spins on its axis, and revolves around the sun.

Chapter 3

MORE SIMPLE PREDICTIONS: THE FOSSIL RECORD AND THE HISTORY OF LIFE

THE BASIC NOTION THAT LIFE HAS EVOLVED PASSES ITS severest test with flying colors: the underlying chemical uniformity of life, and the myriad patterns of special similarities shared by smaller groups of more closely related organisms, all point to a grand pattern of "descent with modification." As if this were not enough, there are still other predictions we can make *if* the basic idea that life has evolved is true. What leaps to mind first—because it is a favorite creationist topic—is the general sequence of life preserved over a span of 3.5 billion years in the fossil record.

As evolutionists, we would predict that simpler forms of life would appear earlier in the fossil record than more advanced forms. This is precisely what we find. The dates and historical information about fossils that confirm this prediction are themselves well-confirmed. When I say that the earliest fossils are about 3.5 billion years old and are primitive forms of algae and bacteria, I am not asserting a literal truth. I mean that one or more scientists have collected hunks of the Warrawoona Group of rocks in northwestern Australia, brought them to the laboratory, sliced them into wafer-thin pieces, and examined, under an ordinary microscope, the filamentous pieces strewn through the rock. They saw a striking similarity between the filaments and modern blue-green algae and other forms of bacteria.

Geologists dated the Warrawoona by applying the techniques of radiometric dating. Ancient sediments are not suitable for this purpose (see Chapter 5), so they analyzed the age of formation of the igneous rocks (lavas) interbedded with the sedimentary layers of the Warrawoona. Their results consistently yielded a date of approximately 3.5 billion years—the age of formation of the Warrawoona. All such dates and facts about the fossil record are there for anyone to recheck. Given the funds and interest, anyone can obtain a piece of the Warrawoona, cut it up and compare its fossils with modern algae. And if radiochemical dating of the associated igneous rocks is a bit beyond the capabilities of most of us, in principle anyone with the proper equipment and know-how can check the results already in. Thus, what sounds like a litany of absolutely authoritative dates and facts is, in reality, a thick compendium of analyses of simple earthly materials that can be rechecked and reanalyzed at will. From this perspective, it soon becomes obvious that the general direction of evolution we deduce from examining modern organisms (from bacteria to timber wolves) is exactly what is found in the historical sequence preserved in the rocks. And all of the dates and interpretations of fossils are as well-confirmed and easily rechecked as the Warrawoona example.

As I pointed out earlier, the oldest rocks known so far are granites from Greenland. Dated at approximately 3.8 billion years, they fall far short of the estimated 4.5 billion years since the birth of the earth. This is as James Hutton, a Scottish farmer and physician, predicted in the 1790s when he wrote of the vast vistas of geologic time. Hutton saw "no vestige of a beginning, no prospect of an end" for the earth. The continuous recycling of the earth's crust, where erosion begins to attack a rock as soon as it is formed and exposed to the ravages of wind and water, preclude any chance of finding *the* primordial granite. The moon, having lost its thin atmosphere at an early age, *does* preserve its earliest rocks on its surface—hence the date, as predicted, of 4.5 billion years of the oldest of the samples brought back by the astronauts.

The Warrawoona Group are the oldest sedimentary rocks yet found. Formed of particles eroded from still other rocks, it is in such piles of quietly accumulating sediments that the bones and shells of dead organisms become entombed. Some of these, in various states of alteration, survive the eons to become the fossilized remnants of life's remote past. The astonishing thing about the rather drab and nondescript blue-green algae (which are really a form of bacteria) is their *extreme* age. The oldest rocks yet found are 3.8 billion years old, the oldest *sedimentary* rocks, at 3.5 billion years, are only slightly younger—and these are already teeming with life. Evidently life is as intrinsic a feature of the earth as are its lands and seas, its mountains and its oceanic trenches.

Bacteria are prokaryotes—single-celled creatures whose chemical machinery of reproduction (the famous DNA) is not housed in a discrete nucleus in the center of the cell. For the next two billion years or so, the only forms of life that show up in the fossil record are these same simple bacteria, though they come in a multiplicity of forms. It was not until about 1.3 billion years ago that the eukaryotes appeared—true algae, with more highly organized cells housing discrete nuclei, the sort of cells we have by the billions in our own bodies. There are today scores of fundamentally different kinds (phyla) of single-celled eukaryotes, most of them living in the oceans. Some are animal-like (such as amoebas and their shelled relatives, the foraminiferans) and others photosynthesize like true plants, the common forms of algae being the most familiar. The fossil record beginning about 1.3 billion years ago provides only a glimpse of this tremendous proliferation of life, a diversification that is still under-appreciated simply because nearly the entire cast of characters is microscopic.

We find the remains of the earliest known large-bodied animals in rocks about 700 million years old. From places as far-flung as Australia, Newfoundland, England, Siberia, and South Africa a strange fauna of soft-bodied creatures has recently come to light. Most of these animals belong to the coral and jellyfish phylum—the coelenterates, whose conical bodies consist of simple tissues not organized into definite organs (such as hearts, gills or stomachs). Some of these fossils are enormous, up to seven feet in length. Some resemble modern jellyfish, while others are sea pens, plumaceous arrays rooted to the sea floor and still very much with us today. Others are like nothing known to haunt the ocean depths in modern times. This as-semblage of soft-bodied animals also contains some wormlike fossils and even the first members of the rather advanced echinoderm phylum, which includes sea urchins and starfish in our modern oceans.

Then there was something of an explosion. Begin-ning about six hundred million years ago, and continu-ing for about ten to fifteen million years, the earliest known representatives of the major kinds of animals still populating today's seas made a rather abrupt appearance. This rather protracted "event" shows up graphically in the rock record: all over the world, at roughly the same time, thick sequences of rocks, barren of any easily detected fossils, are overlain by sediments containing a gorgeous array of shelly invertebrates: trilobites (extinct relatives of crabs and insects), bra-chiopods, mollusks. All of the typical forms of hard-shelled animals we see in the modern oceans appeared, albeit in primitive, prototypical form, in the seas of six hundred million years ago.

Creationists have made much of this sudden develop-ment of a rich and varied fossil record where, just before, there was none. Ignoring its extreme antiquity and accepting, for the moment, the principle that overlying rocks are younger than those lying beneath them (a point creationists deny in other contexts), creationists are fond of asserting that the so-called Cambrian proliferation of life is an instance of the grand episode of Creation. Where is the slow, steady evolution of one life form to another? they ask. Where are the "intermediate forms"? To creationists, the Cambrian episode falsifies the very notion of evolution and bespeaks, instead, the separate acts of a Creator.

Indeed, the sudden appearance of a varied, well-preserved array of fossils, which geologists have used to mark the beginnings of the Cambrian Period (the oldest division of the Paleozoic Era), does pose a fascinating intellectual challenge. Early geologists simply documented the pattern. But, in the years following Darwin's convincing argument establishing "descent with modification," the sudden advent of complex life in the fossil record demanded some sort of explanation. The creationists today, as in so many of their pronouncements, are merely echoing a solution to an intellectual problem current in science several generations ago: *If* life has evolved, as Darwin has said, how can such a proliferation of vastly different life forms appear so suddenly? Doesn't this "Cambrian explosion" flatly falsify the very idea of evolution? The trick, here, is in the phrase "as Darwin said." Creationists confound Darwin's assertion that life has evolved with Darwin's specific ideas on *how* life evolved, and the sorts of patterns he consequently expected to find in the fossil record.

Darwin did indeed project a vista of slow, steady, progressive change. In his day, it was a temerity to suggest that the earth was older than a few millions of years. Darwin ventured to ascribe many millions of years to the earth's antiquity. There was good circumstantial evidence for it—but, more than that, he *needed* what then seemed to be a vast amount of time for his notions of how evolution works to hold.

Taking Darwin's specific view of a slow, stately pace of evolutionary change, from simple to complex, from primitive to advanced, the sudden appearance of a rich and dense fossil record struck everyone as an anomaly. The usual way out was to deny that the fossil record was sufficiently complete to give us a real picture of the pace and pattern of evolutionary change. Thus, geologists and paleontologists of past generations spoke eloquently of the ravages of time, the erosion and metamorphism that destroyed the older vestiges of the fossil record. Life *must* have had a far longer history, allowing for the slow development of primitive to complex prior to the sudden appearance of so many well-differentiated life forms at the beginning of the Cambrian Period.

But who, besides Darwin, said that the tempo of life's evolutionary change must conform to the slow, steady tick of a metronome? The fashion these days is to take the fossil record a bit more literally than before: if we assume, for argument's sake, that the fossil record accurately portrays the gross patterns of the history of life, what does this Cambrian explosion signify? Why, simply that some episodes in evolution proceed faster than others. We have been looking at the fossil record as a general test of the notion that life has evolved: to falsify that general idea, we would have to show that forms of life we considered more advanced appear earlier than simpler forms. Up to this point, we have seen precisely the opposite: more primitive forms antedate more advanced. The Cambrian explosion does not upset this generality. What we see is the nearly simultaneous appearance of many different kinds of hard-shelled organisms—not an inverted sequence of advanced forms preceding simpler forebears.

The Cambrian evolutionary explosion is still shrouded in mystery. Recent detailed explorations of thick Siberian deposits have shown that the "event" may have taken as long as fifteen million years: the "explosion" wasn't the instantaneous, sudden, switching-on earlier geologists (and today's creationists) take it to be. But even fifteen million years seems rather dramatically short for the deployment of most of the phyla of marine life. One recent suggestion is that the level of atmospheric oxygen rose to a critical point so that the oxygen dissolved in sea water finally became sufficient to support a large array of active animal life. Red beds—rocks with a high content of oxidized iron— only go back as far as about two billion years, supporting the notion that, even earlier, the earth's atmosphere was virtually devoid of oxygen. Free oxygen is found as a by-product of photosynthesis, and it has been suggested that it took several billions of years of the photosynthesis of algae to produce the oxygen necessary to support complex animal life. Such a hypothesis is difficult to test, of course, and the real truth underlying this, perhaps the greatest of all events in life's eventful history, may never be nailed down as tightly as one might wish.

But it is the pattern that interests us most here. And if the fossil record tells us anything about evolutionary pattern, it is that some episodes of diversification can happen so rapidly that no detailed, stratified record showing the gradual development from primitive to advanced is ever formed. Darwin felt that such a pattern, if taken literally, threatened his very notion of evolution—and indeed creationists still claim it does. What Darwin, and the creationists, have confused is the basic notion that evolution has occurred with the various possible ways in which evolution might conceivably happen. The fossil record seems to be telling us, first, that the general sequence of life is consistent with the general notion of evolution, and second, that rare events such as the Cambrian explosion are at the very least not inconsistent with the idea that life has evolved. As we shall soon see when we examine some contemporary controversies in evolutionary theory, the fossil record also suggests to some of us that some of the specific ideas that Darwin, and many of his successors right up to the present day, had on how life evolves may well be at least partly wrong.

The rest of life's history in the sea—the whole six hundred million years of it—is a story rich in detail but simple in outline. The same general sorts of life (worms, corals, arthropods [trilobites, crustaceans], clams, snails, and fish of various sorts) have filled the seas from day one, so to speak. But the specific cast of characters has changed, and the numerical dominance of some older groups has given way to others in the course of time. For example, the dominant "shellfish"—bivalved animals living on the sea bottom—in the Paleozoic Era (600–240 million years ago) were the brachiopods. Today the clams, superficially similar but only remotely related to brachiopods, dominate, while the brachiopods, now greatly reduced in number, cower in crevices in and among rocky coastlines and coral reefs.

Such changes have not been graceful. The grand theme in life's past six hundred million years has been peaceful coexistence, occasionally violently disrupted by major episodes of extinction that appear to have eliminated seventy-five percent or more or all species in some cases. Such events—the most famous terminating the Paleozoic and Mesozoic Eras (when the dinosaurs finally died out)—took upward of a million years to accomplish. But, once again, such long periods show up as dramatically sudden turnovers if the rock record is taken literally. One can go to Upper Cretaceous marine deposits in Denmark and Italy, for example, and trace the continued existence of typical Cretaceous species of marine life right up to the point where they all seem to drop out. Just above the last Cretaceous fossils, in chalky limestones of the same character and consistency, one finds a smaller array of rather different species. The cast of characters is always different, but the outline of the story is always the same: for real change to accrue in life's past six hundred million years, wholesale housecleaning always preceded a reproliferation. The newly recovered biota (animals and plants) always looked somewhat different from its predecessor: some lineages would escape extinction and, finding new opportunities, themselves proliferate into a host of new species—a group which a paleontologist, coming along millions of years later, would designate as an entire new family or order. Rather than stately progression, the gross history of life shows a mixture of status quo and revolution. But the *order* is there: those organisms we think are more advanced than others (bees and ants, say, over dragonflies) show up in the expected order as fossils: dragonflies are fairly common in lake deposits of 280 million years ago, while ants and bees don't show up until the Mesozoic, over one hundred million years later.

Being vertebrates ourselves, it is with the fish, amphibians, reptiles, and mammals that we are most interested. Here the fossil record has, in a sense, been deceiving, because the vertebrates conform to Darwin's expectations far better than any other group: "fishes" of various sorts predate the earliest vertebrates to clamber out on land—"amphibians," which were still obliged to return to the water to reproduce (as frogs and salamanders do today). The development of the amniote egg, which presented the developing embryo with its own protected, watery environment, came later, and the reptiles, creatures that first possessed such eggs, came after the first amphibians. Birds and mammals, both in a sense simply highly derived versions of the two basic, early types of reptiles, came even later. The sequence is clear, an evolutionist's delight—though, in a way, our infatuation with the superficially gradual nature of vertebrate evolution has tended to blind evolutionary biologists to the more usual pattern of stasis punctuated by occasional revolutions—the normal pattern of historical change for the bulk of life.

We have spent enough time on the basic features of

the fossil record to illustrate two points on which most paleontologists and geologists agree: the fossil record abundantly affirms the general notion that life has evolved, but it calls into question some of our more time-honored and long-accepted ideas about the pace and general mode of evolutionary change—"evolutionary theory," properly speaking. The creationists, of course, are well aware of this and have exploited the situation to the hilt.

Chapter 4

HOW LIFE HAS EVOLVED: THE EVOLUTION OF EVOLUTIONARY THEORY

IF LIFE HAS EVOLVED, AND IF SOME KINDS OF EVOLU-
tionary change can happen sufficiently rapidly to be
observed during one person's lifetime, we should be
able to go to nature to observe the change, to measure
its tempo, and to test ideas about how and why it happens. And we should be able to simulate some kinds of
evolutionary change experimentally on laboratory organisms, and even use mathematics and computers to
run evolutionary experiments on an even more abstract
level. In fact, all of these activities have been vigor-
ously pursued for well over a century now, and form
the basis of the general subject of evolutionary biology.
It is not the question, Has life evolved? that motivates
such study; it is the question, *How* has life evolved?
that forms the central focus of such research. That
breeders can radically alter the anatomical and behavioral properties of domestic animals, and geneticists
can experimentally alter their fruit flies and guinea pigs,
shows that small-scale evolutionary change can and
does take place in short intervals of time—a circumstance consistent with the general notion of evolution.
Creationists concede such small-scale changes are possible, but deny that they are the stuff of large-scale

change between "basic kinds"—a point we will return to later.

One of the more ironic aspects of the current upsurge in creationism is that it coincides almost exactly with the first major period of activity in evolutionary theory in nearly fifty years. Evolution itself has been attracting a great deal of attention from a wide assortment of biologists, and the current healthy controversy in which evolutionary biology is now embroiled has spilled over into the media even without the added cachet of creationist attacks. Superficially, it looks as if we know less now about how evolution works than we did, say, even ten years ago. This is because as recently as a decade ago there was something approaching unanimity in the evolutionary ranks. Today, though chaos is too strong a word, there is definitely dissent in the ranks. Few biologists agree as completely and complacently as they did that short time ago. Creationists see this and have been quick to react. Their basic conclusion is that evolutionary biologists can't even agree among themselves, so who would want their dangerous and ill-supported notions taught as "fact" in public schools?

What this charge amounts to, of course, is that evolutionary biologists—geneticists, developmental biologists, systematists, and paleontologists—stand convicted, guilty . . . of doing science. On the contrary, research in evolutionary biology today is actually a textbook case of just how it is that science is supposed to operate. The unusual thing about evolutionary biology is not its current state of flux. If anything was unusual, it was perhaps the period of quiescence and agreement from which evolutionary biology is only now beginning to emerge.

Arkansas Statute 590, signed into law by Governor Frank D. White on March 19, 1981, defines "evolution-science" in part as the acceptance of "the sufficiency of mutation and natural selection in bringing about development of present living kinds from simple earlier kinds." All biologists realize that there is more to the evolutionary process than simply mutation and natural selection. For example, when new species arise from old, a period of geographic isolation is usually considered necessary to disrupt the reproductive continuity which binds the members of a species together. Thus the statute is in error, as no biologist ever took the extreme position that mutation and natural selection alone suffice to account for the evolution of all living things.

But it *is* true that evolutionary biology, approximately since the time of the Scopes trial, has embraced a starkly simple view of how life evolves. And, to be sure, natural selection has lain at the very heart of this, the so-called synthetic theory. When the English biologist Julian Huxley published *Evolution, The Modern Synthesis* in 1942, he coined a name for the body of thought that derived its strength and appeal from its simplicity: the synthesis (I'll omit the word "modern" since it isn't, particularly, anymore) put together the ideas of genetics with Darwin's older views on adaptation through natural selection. Most biologists saw the logical appeal, and paleontologists and systematists began to claim that the evolutionary patterns they saw in their plants and animals were consistent with the simple mechanisms of change envisioned by the new genetics.

Thus the heart of modern evolutionary theory to the present day was forged in the late 1920s and early 1930s, and "neodarwinism" was born. Neodarwinian theory differs from Darwin's original notions only in the sense that now, i.e., in the early 1930s, there was a theory of inheritance (genetics) of which Darwin had been wholly ignorant. Darwin did know a few basic things about heredity. He knew that offspring tend to resemble their parents and grandparents. And he knew that the resemblance was not precise. Only some sets of twins were ever identical. And from time to time, offspring would appear with strikingly novel features.

Darwin's views on why all this was so belong in the same realm of outmoded scientific concepts as the idea of a flat earth, or the notion that the sun revolves around our planet. His theory of inheritance envisioned various organs of the body each contributing "gemmules," little forerunners of each different cell type in the body, which congregate in eggs and sperm and develop into parental replicas in the offspring. We now know that the same information that serves as a recipe for development in the fertilized egg is found in *each* of the billions of cells in any vertebrate's body. Darwin knew nothing of this, but as it turned out, his ignorance was sublimely irrelevant to the problem he was really interested in tackling—evolution. Reading economists and other social theorists of his day, he became entranced with the observation that resources—food and other forms of energy—were typically in short supply for humankind. There always seemed to be some sort of balance between supply and demand, but as Darwin read in Thomas Malthus' *Essay on Population,* if every child survived to adulthood, the population would soon outstrip all available resources. Clearly this never happens. The vision of vast numbers of children failing to survive long enough to reproduce was all Darwin needed to combine with what he knew to be true of patterns of heredity in order to come up with the notion of natural selection. He may not have understood *why* organisms resemble their parents, *why* there is variation within a population at each generation, or *why* offspring sometimes have strikingly novel characteristics. But he did know that these things were so. Darwin explained as an inexorable law of nature the fact that fewer offspring survive to form the succeeding generation than are actually born: in the competition for limited resources, those organisms best suited to coping with the rigors of their environment will prevail. *They* will tend to survive, and their progeny—which on the whole resemble them—will retain the virtues that impart success, and then pass them on to succeeding generations. To each generation, the environment poses harsh challenges, and not all individuals will survive. Among the variations in the population, only those best suited will make it.

Herbert Spencer, a Victorian social theorist, dubbed natural selection "survival of the fittest," and Alfred Lord Tennyson spoke of "nature red in tooth and claw." It *was* rather a horrific, fiercely competitive, devil-take-the-hindmost vision. Its materialism bothered Darwin as much as anyone else. But he stuck to his guns, as he saw no other way to explain evolutionary change. And his arguments were so successful that his 1859 *On the Origin of Species* persuaded most biologists and geologists, and a substantial segment of the nonscientific public, that evolution must have occurred. Darwin reviewed all the telltale signs in nature suggesting evolution must have happened. But he convinced the world of the reality of evolution mainly by propounding a simple, believable theory on *how* evolution occurs. Today we are at pains to separate the two: that evolution has occurred is, as we have seen, a proposition that has passed, with flying colors, all reputable attempts to discard it. *How* evolution occurs, however, remains a legitimate area of scientific inquiry and controversy.

Actually, Darwin's vision of natural selection was more catholic even than the version I have just characterized. To Darwin, any form of competition leading to differential success of one group over another was "natural selection." Thus, though competition between individuals within a species was basically what he had in mind when he wrote of "natural selection," competition between groups, or even entire species, also fit in with his rather eclectic notion of natural selection. Indeed, Darwin's *The Origin* was subtitled "Or The Preservation of Favoured Races in the Struggle for Life."

In a profound sense, the storm of controversy in evolution these days is a reaction against the version and perceived role of natural selection that was codified in the 1930s and became rigid in the 1940s and 1950s. When natural selection was refurbished in those days, it was in a rather more narrow sense than Darwin originally meant it: to geneticists then, natural selection meant "differential reproductive success." Gone is the stark vision of individual deaths in the "struggle for life." It has been replaced by the gentler vision of a competition simply to leave more genes to the next generation. Those animals and plants that prove more vigorous, more hardy, will on the whole be the ones that flourish and reproduce themselves, forming the succeeding generation.

If natural selection was somewhat defanged by this sophisticated rendition, the concept was also considerably narrowed. From the 1930s onward, natural selection has been limited, as an idea, only to reproductive competition between individuals within a species—an idea Darwin had firmly in mind, but not the only competitive scenario he originally included under "natural selection." This restricted version of natural selection forms the core of the synthetic theory of evolution, and it is the extremely important role accorded to this rather limited notion of natural selection which lies at the heart of most of the controversy in evolutionary biology these days.

The Advent of Genetics

Darwin touched off a storm when he published *The Origin*. Today's creationism is, in some sense, merely an echo of that distant thunder. But many of the biologists who were immediately convinced that life had evolved, took sharp issue with Darwin's notions on *how* life evolved. Natural selection seemed to some a bit too brutish, too materialistic. And still other biologists were attracted to alternative theories on how life might have evolved. Foremost among the competing theories was "Lamarckism."

Jean-Baptiste Lamarck (1744–1829) was a French zoologist active a half century prior to the appearance of Darwin's book. A great zoologist convinced of the interconnectedness of all life, Lamarck is remembered today (largely in scorn) mostly for one tiny fragment of his intellectual edifice: he thought that evolutionary change occurred when an organism developed some new capability, or underwent some slight modification, during the course of its lifetime, and subsequently passed the newly acquired trait along to its offspring. The classic conflicting scenarios of "how the giraffe got its long neck" (with apologies to Rudyard Kipling) demonstrate the differences between the Lamarckian notion of the "inheritance of acquired characteristics" and Darwinian natural selection. The Lamarckian version sees individual proto-giraffes stretching their necks, craning for leaves in tree canopies, and passing on their slightly distended necks to the next generation. The Darwinian view invokes variation in neck length, and imagines a situation where competition for leaves high up in tree canopies selectively favors those proto-giraffes with the relatively longer necks. These tend to survive and leave more offspring, and little by little the average neck size of the proto-giraffe lineage increases.

It is a testimony both to Victorian biology's ignorance of genetics and to the persuasiveness of Lamarckian-inclined biologists that Darwin allowed Lamarckian notions to creep into later edtions of *The Origin*—though he steadfastly maintained his preference for natural selection. But in the 1880s, just after Darwin's death, the German biologist Auguste Weismann propounded what we now call the "Weismann doctrine"—that germ cells (eggs and sperm) create the physical body, and it is a one-way street. Nothing that happens to the body turns around and affects the germ cells. Characteristics developed during an organism's lifetime cannot be transmitted to offspring. Weismann, in other words, claimed to have refuted Lamarckian notions of evolution. *Nature,* one of the more prestigious science journals, recently published a controversial report claiming the experimental verification of the inheritance of an acquired character—in this case, one involving immunological tolerance. Though most biologists are unwilling to go so far as to resurrect Lamarck's notions of evolutionary change, it is a sign of today's unsettled times in evolutionary biology to see one of its most solid underpinnings—Weismann's doctrine—called into question.

In any case, Weismann had convincingly removed Lamarckian notions from biology just when genetics was in its birth throes in the early years of the twentieth century, when three biologists nearly simultaneously discovered the works of the Austrian monk Gregor Mendel (1822–1884). Mendel's famous experiments with peas implied that the factors that underlie the inheritance of features—say blue or brown eyes, or wrinkled or smooth pea skins—were *particulate,* since there was a marked degree of independence and shuffling of these characteristics that seemed to follow simple laws when careful breeding experiments were performed. Within a decade, the science of genetics was up and running, and important discoveries—such as that genes lie in linear arrays on chromosomes in the nuclei of all but the simplest cells—had already been made.

All of the rapid advances made in the heady days of early research in genetics seemed to challenge Darwin's pet idea of natural selection. In fact, most biologists concentrated on such fields as genetics and the equally rapidly advancing field of physiology, spurning evolutionary biology altogether as old-fashioned. And those biologists left to ponder the mysteries of evolution professionally in the early decades of the twentieth century were troubled: How could Darwin's scheme of natural selection working on a smoothly gradational field of variation be reconciled with the idea that genes were separate particles, each producing its own characteris-

tic? And what of the Dutch botanist Hugo deVries'
notion of "mutations"—where large-scale changes in
the flower of the evening primrose would suddenly appear? "Mutations" came to be the official term for
what the breeders had, for years, more informally
termed "sports"—the unexpected, quirky appearance of
new forms *not* inherited from parents, or, for that matter, grandparents. Mutations were the source of all true
novelty, it seemed—but they also seemed to be large-
scale effects, not the minor new forms of variation required by the classical Darwinian view. Again, natural
selection seemed to be in trouble. By the 1920s, biology
had once again drifted rather far from the Darwinian
fold—though evolutionists were quick to rally around
the flag when the call went out for expert witnesses
(who actually never ended up on the stand) for the
Scopes trial.

Thus, just when the Scopes case came bursting onto
the national stage, evolution was a relatively minor area
of biological research taken as a whole, and was fraught
with difficulties. Some paleontologists in the 1920s still
clung to Lamarckian notions (despite Weismann's val-
iant efforts), while others adopted "vitalism"—a mysti-
cal notion that saw evolution as an inner-directed drive
to perfection. But it was the apparent conflict between
genetics and Darwin's notion of natural selection that
was the real stumbling block. And it was the work of
three mathematically gifted geneticists—Sewall Wright,
J. B. S. Haldane, and Sir Ronald Fisher—that resolved
the apparent incongruities between the mechanisms of
inheritance and the principle of natural selection. By
the late 1920s, it had become clear that many mutations had relatively minor effects, that some genes had
a role in forming more than one characteristic, and,
most importantly, that most characters are formed by
the action of more than one gene. The old black/white,
brown/blue, wrinkled/smooth, either/or constraint in
the theory of inheritance had given way to the view
that saw how a spectrum of variation (in height, say, or

number of head hairs) could nonetheless be under genetic control. All of a sudden, there were no longer any formal objections, from the genetics quarter, to the notion of natural selection working to preserve the most beneficial of a spectrum of variation in each generation. All this came from genetics, despite complete ignorance of the biochemical "anatomy" of genes—the structure of DNA. The biochemical basis of inheritance was still a "black box"—but at least what geneticists had learned circa 1930 no longer seemed to render natural selection an impossibility.

The Synthetic Theory

The way was thus cleared for a rapprochement between genetics and evolutionary theory. Wright, Fisher, and Haldane made important contributions. But it was the Russian-born geneticist, Theodosius Dobzhansky, an immigrant to New York in the 1920s, who really put it all together. Trained as a naturalist (actually, as a beetle specialist), Dobzhansky took up the study of fruit flies that had already yielded such stunning experimental results in Thomas Hunt Morgan's laboratory at Columbia University. In the 1930s, Dobzhansky began a long series of studies in the wild of fruit-fly genetics —a series that continued right up to his death in 1975.

In 1937, Dobzhansky published his first major book, *Genetics and the Origin of Species,** a title with a deliberate reference to Darwin's greatest book, published so long before. And the bridge Dobzhansky built involved far more than a literary allusion. In the book, Dobzhansky effectively argued for the central role played by natural selection in changing the genetic composition of populations of organisms in nature. Darwin emerged completely vindicated: natural popu-

* Further information about the works discussed in this book may be found in the Bibliography.

lations seemed to possess ample amounts of genetic variation. But this variation, as Darwin himself had noted, seemed highly organized. Local populations within a species differed from place to place, reflecting adaptation to slightly different environments. The average length of a sparrow's wing, for example, is longer in warmer climes than in populations situated high up the slopes of mountain ranges. The physiological explanation is simple: shorter wings radiate less body heat, a distinct advantage in colder climates. Natural selection, then, preserved those variants within species which were best suited to the precise ecological conditions of each local habitat over the entire range of a species.

Yet Dobzhansky's book is perhaps best remembered for his discussion of yet another aspect of evolution: the origin of new species. Darwin, ironically, never did discuss the origin of species in his book of that name. To Darwin, the origin of species was synonymous with evolution itself. The simple accumulation of anatomical change over thousands and millions of years was what Darwin had in mind when he thought of new species arising from old. Occasionally, he realized, species would somehow become fragmented, so that what was once a single species would leave two (or even more) species, each newly embarked along slowly divergent, separate pathways. But to Darwin, such divergence was little more than a special case of natural selection molding far-flung populations along somewhat different lines, until their differences appeared so great that we would be obliged to call them different species.

On the other hand, Dobzhansky and other biologists in the 1930s recognized that species were something more than mere collections of anatomical and behavioral properties. They were also breeding communities. Years of observation in the field and experience in the lab and breeder's pen, showed that most species couldn't be successfully mated even with their closest relatives. More to the point, even in instances where such hybridization was technically possible—when the species were found together in the wild—hybrids were nonetheless rare, or altogether absent. Even if they could interbreed, they didn't. Lions and tigers in India (yes, there still are a few lions in India) have been in close contact in some places within human memory, yet, insofar as I am aware, the "tiglons" produced in some zoos have never been seen in the wild.

How do new reproductive groups—new species—originate? Dobzhansky's thoughtful discussion of the origin of what he called "isolating mechanisms" appeared to have settled the issue. The behavioral and anatomical differences between species are what keeps them from interbreeding. These differences evolve—or at least begin to appear—usually when a species is so far-flung that some of its populations become isolated from the main group. In other words, normal adaptive differentiation (as with sparrow-wing length), plus prolonged isolation, when no mating between the two divisions of a species takes place, starts the ball rolling. *If* divergence has gone on far enough—when the two groups which used to be members of the same species once again come into contact—it may be that they can no longer interbreed.

Ernst Mayr, an ornithologist working at the American Museum of Natural History in New York, published *Systematics and the Origin of Species* a few years after Dobzhansky's book appeared. Mayr knew that naturalists even before Darwin were aware of a general pattern in nature in which a species' closest relative typically lived in some adjacent region, and not in the same area. Victorian naturalists called such species "vicars" (in the sense that they either replaced or represented one another geographically) or "geminate" ("twin") species. In a sense, such species were just slightly different versions of the same thing. The scarlet tanager of eastern North America, for example, is "replaced" in the west by the equally striking, if differently colored, western tanager.

Darwin used the evidence of geographic variation and vicariant species as part of his argument that life must have evolved. Dobzhansky, Mayr, and other evolutionists of the 1930s and 1940s were emphasizing the importance (in fact, the utter necessity) of geographic isolation to disrupt an ancestral species to produce two species where once there had been but one. Evolution was descent with modification all right, but it was produced by a one–two combination of adaptive change plus occasional episodes of disruption, producing the great array of different species we see all around us today. And of the two, it was adaptive change that seemed clearly the most important. Natural selection, patiently favoring the best of a spectrum of variants, accounts for the behavioral and anatomical change we see in evolution. And it is because such change is constantly going on that populations will further diverge when geographically isolated. So Darwin was right all along, the origin of species is ultimately a function of adaptive change through natural selection, with the slight added factor of physical separation needed to sunder a species into two reproductively isolated, separate species. Now, by the early 1940s, we had a theory about how natural selection effects genetic change, and how accumulated genetic change plus geographic isolation yields reproductive isolation—new species.

But what of the large-scale changes in evolution? Neodarwinism spoke directly to the evolution of the sorts of differences between, say, lions and tigers. The conclusion that the kind of adaptive change *within* species underlies the differences we see *between* closely related species seemed so voluminous and incontestable that even today's creationists accept microevolution. (This is the creationist admission that there is variation, including the origin of new reproductively isolated species, within "basic kinds" that we will examine shortly). Patterns of evolutionary change within species seemed no different in principle—just milder in degree—from the sorts of changes we see between closely related species. All evolutionary changes were produced by natural selection working each generation on the variation presented to it. Could this simple process also account for *all* the changes among the larger groups of animals and plants?

Closely related species are classified in the same genus, and related genera are put in the same family. Families are lumped together in the same order, while related orders are grouped into the same class. This is the Linnaean hierarchy that was devised, long before Darwin's day, to hold the nested pattern of similarities that define groups of organisms, a pattern naturalists had observed in the organic world since Aristotle. But what *are* these genera, families, orders and so on? It was clear to Darwin, and should be obvious to all today, that they are simply ever-larger categories used to give names to ever-larger clusters of related species. That's *all* they are—simply clusters of related species. Thus, in principle, the evolution of a family should be no different in its basic nature, and should involve no different processes, than the evolution of a genus, since a family is nothing more than a collection of related genera. And genera are just collections of related species. The triumph of evolutionary biology in the 1930s and 1940s was the conclusion that the same principles of adaptive divergence going on within species produce the differences we see between closely related species—i.e., within genera. Q.E.D.: If adaptive modification within species explains the evolutionary differences between species within a genus, logically it must explain *all* the evolutionary change we see between families, orders, classes, phyla, and the kingdoms of life.

This highly reasonable inference still demanded cogent exposition. In his *Tempo and Mode in Evolution* (a book begun in the late 1930s, but not published until 1944), George Gaylord Simpson—a vertebrate paleontologist also at the American Museum—attempted to show that all the major changes in life's evolutionary history could be understood as a by-product of the newly understood principles of genetic change. To do so, he had to confront that greatest and most persistent of paleontological bugbears: the notorious gaps of the fossil record.

The Synthesis and the Fossil Record

Darwin and his evolution-minded successors in the paleontological ranks preferred to explain these gaps away: they blamed the incompleteness of the geologic record of the events of earth history. According to this explanation, the lack of abundant (creationists say "any") examples of smoothly gradational change between ancestors and descendants in the fossil record merely bears witness to the gaps in the quality of the rock record. Not entirely so, said Simpson, to his everlasting credit.

Simpson thought the fossil record had a great deal to say about how evolution occurred—its pace and style, its "tempo and mode." After all, it is in the enormous expanse of geologic time that the evolutionary game has actually been played. But to make a such a claim is also to assert that the fossil record is at least complete enough to be taken seriously. Thus the gaps had to be confronted. And since gaps there certainly are, they must at least in part be a *product* of the evolutionary process if they were not merely the artifacts of a poor geologic record.

It is the gaps in the fossil record which, perhaps more than any other facet of the natural world, are dearly beloved by creationists. As we shall see when we take up the creationist position, there are all sorts of gaps: absence of gradationally intermediate "transitional" forms between species, but also between larger groups—between, say, families of carnivores, or the orders of mammals. In fact, the higher up the Linnaean hierarchy you look, the fewer transitional forms there seem to be. For example, *Peripatus,* a lobe-legged, wormlike creature that haunts rotting logs in the Southern Hemisphere, appears intermediate in many respects between two of the major phyla on earth today—the segmented worms and the arthropods. But few other phyla have such intermediates with other phyla, and when we scan the fossil record for them we find some, but basically little, help. Extinction has surely weeded out many of the intermediate species, but on the other hand, the fossil record is not exactly teeming with their remains.

Simpson knew this, but preferred a view of evolution consistent with the emerging principles of genetic change over the alternative posed by German paleontologist Otto Schindewolf. Schindewolf interpreted the gaps in the fossil record as evidence of the sudden appearance of new groups of animals and plants. Not a creationist, Schindewolf believed all forms of life to be interrelated, but felt that the fossil record implied a *saltational* mode—literally, sudden jumps from one basic type (called a *Bauplan,* or fundamental architectural design—conceptually if tangentially related to creationists' "basic kinds"). Simpson and his peers scoffed at such an idea, and rightly so, as there was little evidence emanating from genetics laboratories that even remotely hinted at how such sudden leaps could occur. And the cardinal rule of science—that all ideas must be testable—held sway: the prevailing theory and evidence of genetics of the 1930s—and it hasn't changed all that much today—was against large-scale, sudden switches in the physical appearance of descendant organisms. Schindewolf's views were at odds with nearly all that was known of genetics in the 1930s. His saltational explanation of the gaps was impressive—but wrong, as far as Simpson was concerned.

Simpson thought that most of the fossil record amply supported Darwin's view. There was plenty of evidence, he felt, to show that ninety percent of evolution involved the gradual transition from one species to the next through time. When there were gaps between closely related species and genera—in other words, when new species appeared abruptly in the fossil record with no smoothly intergradational intermediates between them and their ancestors—he was content to blame it on the vagaries of preservation inherent in the fossil record. This, of course, was the standard cry invented long before Simpson's time. (It will spoil nothing of this narrative to say that today I, and numerous colleagues in the field of paleontology, don't accept this explanation—hence some of the current controversy.) But Simpson did acknowledge that the sudden appearance of new groups—those ranked rather high in the Linnaean hierarchy, and to some extent what the creationists call "basic kinds"—implies something *real* about how evolution works. If evolution was always a slow, steady change from species to species, Simpson pointed out, the transitions between major groups would typically take millions of years, and we should expect to find some fossil evidence of the transitional forms. Not finding them very often, he deduced, implied that evolution sometimes went on rather quickly—in brief, intense spurts. The presence of *some* intermediates (such as *Archaeopteryx,* the proto-bird) falsified Schindewolf's saltational notions. But the relative scarcity of such intermediates bespoke a major mode of evolution producing truly rapid change—a mode Simpson called "quantum evolution."

In physics, a "quantum" is a sudden, definite shift in state, an either–or proposition. The fossil record mimics these sudden changes in state as, for instance, the evolution of whales from terrestrial mammalian forebears. Whales first appeared in the Eocene, some fifty-five million years ago. They are primitive—for whales. But the earliest specimens *look* like whales, and it is only their general mammalian features that tell us they must have sprung from some other group of terrestrial mammals in the Paleocene. Bats are another example: a perfect specimen from the Eocene of Wyoming is primitive—for bats. But anyone looking at it will see at once that it is a bat, and evidence for its derivation from some particular kind of insectivorous Paleocene mammal still hasn't turned up as yet.

Simpson's specific theory about how these sudden shifts come about in the course of evolution is no longer accepted in all its details—the main reason being that Simpson himself effectively retracted the idea in a later book published in 1953. The original idea of "quantum evolution" envisioned a small population rapidly losing the adaptations of its parental species, going through a shaky phase, and then luckily hitting on a new set of anatomical and behavioral features suitable to life in a new—radically new—ecological niche. Simpson supported his theoretical stance with the solid structure of genetics, but later dropped the notions of an "inadaptive" and "preadaptive" phase. Why he did so reveals the power of the very idea of natural selection.

The tide of thinking in genetics was simply running against notions of genetic change that didn't specifically include natural selection. Early in the 1930s, for instance, the geneticist Sewall Wright spoke about competition between breeding populations (he called them "demes") within a species and of the role chance plays in determining the composition of the next generation. Wright was not wholly infatuated with natural selection as the only agent of evolutionary change. Although his concept of "genetic drift" as a random factor in evolution was accepted by his peers, it was a grudging acceptance. It is only recently that his "shifting balance theory," where the differential success of demes is the major issue, has once again begun to be taken seriously. Both notions pay but little heed to the narrow, restricted version of natural selection, which is differential reproductive success of individuals within demes based on their relative abilities to cope with life's exigencies. But by and large, Dobzhansky's book, plus Mayr's and Simpson's and a host of shorter technical publications in the late 1930s and 1940s, came close to asserting that the only truly significant force underlying genetic, hence evolutionary, change is natural selection. By 1953, Simpson himself saw his original concept of quantum evolution as too far removed from the consensus. He modified quantum evolution to mean merely an extremely rapid phase of change, governed throughout by natural selection as a small population invaded a new habitat.

By the early 1950s, the synthesis, as we know it today, was complete. It said that genetic change is largely a function of natural selection working on a field of variation presented to it each generation. *New* features from time to time appear, ultimately brought about by mutation. Most mutations are harmful; some are neutral, or even beneficial. The neutral or beneficial ones hang on, and one day might prove to be a real advantage as the environment provides new challenges to the organisms. In any case, as the environment changes, as all environments eventually do, it does so slowly. Natural selection preserves the best of each generation, and their genes make up the succeeding generation. Through time, through enough generations, selection wreaks tremendous changes. And occasionally habitats divide and species fragment, following separate adaptive histories. Hence, species multiply. Given enough time—and remember that geologists tell us that the earth is fully 4.5 billion years old—all manner of change will accrue. This, in a nutshell, is the synthetic theory of evolution. Though probably right in most essentials, it appears to an increasing number of contemporary biologists to be inaccurate in some respects—some, perhaps, even major respects. Hence, today's controversy—whch should chill, rather than gladden, creationists' hearts. And at the center of today's evolutionary wranglings, we have the by-now familiar "force": natural selection.

Modern Controversies (1) Nondarwinian Evolution

One of the older arguments in genetics concerns the amount of genetic variation actually present in wild populations. Some geneticists thought quite a lot of variability must be there, but many reputable geneticists for years thought in terms of a simple system of two or three forms ("alleles") per gene. One allele would be dominant, the other recessive. Though it was widely acknowledged that there was much more variation at some genetic loci than this simple picture suggests, no one was really prepared for the astonishing new evidence on genetic variability that began to appear in the 1960s. With the invention of electrophoresis, where a slight electrical charge separates proteins along a paper strip, geneticists all of a sudden had a simple way of seeing variation in the structure of individual proteins—implying variation in the parts of the genetic code responsible for producing each enzyme (protein). Electrophoresis became all the rage, and it soon developed that most populations contained far more genetic variation than most geneticists had ever imagined. The problem then became: How could all this variation be consistent with natural selection, which supposedly inexorably favors only the best of the field of possible variants?

The theory of natural selection has always recognized that there may well be two or more different "solutions" to the same engineering problem. Take eyes, for example. Many animal groups have developed eyes independently. Arthropods, such as insects and crustaceans, have utilized their hard outer skeletons to fashion a system of multiple lenses. The lenses trap light and focus it on photoreceptors beneath the external lenses. We vertebrates, with our internal skeletons, had to take another approach to the problem. Our eyes are like pinhole cameras, where light passes through an adjustable aperture, and then passes through an onion-shaped internal lens, thus focusing on the retina. Two different solutions to the same problem: vision. Yet squids and octopi, far more closely related to arthropods and annelid worms (as judged, for example, on patterns of intricate similarity of the larval development in all three groups), nonetheless have eyes far more similar to ours than to the compound eyes of fleas and shrimp. Also lacking a hard outer skeleton around their heads, squid and octopus eyes are also built along pinhole-camera principles and, superficially at least, look very much like vertebrate eyes. Multiple solutions there may be, but there is always a limit, usually a rather small number of designs that can accomplish the same biological function.

Thus theory predicts that natural selection will favor, say, two or three equally viable "solutions" to a functional biological problem. But how can natural selection have failed to "see" that some of the many variant forms of particular proteins are better than others? For that was what geneticists involved with electrophoresis were forced to conclude: most of those genetic variants they were detecting with their apparatus *must* be as "good" as one another. *All* the variant protein forms fit into the chemical machinery of the cell. For example, fruit flies have an enzyme—"xanthine dehydrogenase" —which comes in over twenty different versions. All must work equally well, or natural selection would have eliminated the less efficient forms long ago.

Natural selection is "saved" as a concept if we assume that all these alternative forms of gene products are equally viable. But in so arguing, the all-encompassing importance of natural selection is somewhat diminished. In the 1960s, "nondarwinian evolution," or the theory of "neutrality," simply said that nature was far more tolerant of variation than the modern synthesis had ever imagined—or seemed prepared to tolerate. Strict selectionists reacted with horror to this breach in the bastion of natural selection:

If natural selection could not "see" the differences between all these alternate gene forms, how could we explain the differences in these genes between closely related species? "Neutralists" began openly to speak of the importance of random effects in evolution: if a mutation occurs, and the slightly modified protein that results is equally as good at performing its function as the previously established forms, that new mutant may well survive. At the very least, it won't be removed by natural selection. A view of a sort of "molecular clock" with a statistically regular "ticking" of random change was developed—a view that specifically denies that natural selection can have any real control over rates of evolutionary change amid the array of equally viable alternative forms of specific proteins in organisms' cells.

Today, such nondarwinian notions of biochemical change have been incorporated into the mainstream of biological thought. But though it is no longer particularly controversial, nondarwinian evolution is noteworthy not only as an advance in understanding, but also because it was the first of many recent challenges to the previously conventional view of the supreme power and importance of natural selection as the main agent of evolutionary change. Modern molecular genetics is almost daily turning up surprising new information about how the genetic code is organized and how its messages are translated into adult offspring. Here, too, we find additional challenges to the ability of natural selection to govern all evolutionary modifications in the process of development from egg to adult. No one disputes that developmental pathways *must* be modified for evolution to occur. But, again, it is *how* such modifications happen that all the fighting is about. And, again, proponents of the supreme importance of natural selection seem impelled to give way a bit even here, and admit that other factors, such as the strict mechanical problems of producing tissues and organs from a single mass of proliferating cells, are also at play.

(2) More Problems from the Fossil Record

Another source of controversy in recent years has come from some students of the fossil record. For years, as we have seen, paleontologists have agreed that the simple formulations of genetics are consistent with evolutionary change seen in the fossil record. And we have also seen that the gross pattern of such change is far more episodic than might be expected from a straightforward application of Darwinian principles—a pattern that Simpson addressed with his notion of quantum evolution in the 1940s.

But in the 1970s, paleontologists began to question Simpson's assertion that fully ninety percent of the evolutionary patterns between fossil species were of the slow, steady, gradual sort predicted by Darwin and his intellectual descendants. The fundamental observation was there for all to see: anyone familiar with the fossil record of, say, marine invertebrates, knows that new species appear from time to time. And one can collect them at different levels in the rocks of a region. Many of these fossils persist for long periods of time, yet tend to remain most definitely, and recognizably, the same. One trilobite I know especially well lived in the inland seas of North America from about 370 to 360 million years ago. (The dates are estimates based on radiochemical dating of igneous rocks intruding into sedimentary rocks containing similar fossils elsewhere.)

During its ten-million-year sojourn, this trilobite group produced several new species. But the pattern was as episodic as the grosser patterns of change that we have already seen fill the fossil record. The oldest, most primitive species inhabited the limy seas in the center of the continent and hung on unchanged for about four million years. It did not slowly transform into its descendant: in fact, its descendant species arose along the eastern margin of the continent soon after the stock became established. There is one quarry (in cen-

tral New York State) that so far has produced intermediates between the two species. Once evolved, the
descendant species lived on for the entire remaining
time-span of the group—about eight million years. The
primitive ancestral species disappeared when the seas
themselves disappeared from the continental interior;
when once again the seas returned, it was the descendant, already well-established for several million years
in the east, that came in with it. Collecting these
trilobites in the midwest, then, shows the ancestor
persisting through a sequence of rocks representing
several millions of years. Suddenly, as we go up the
rock column, the descendant species appears. There is
no evidence of slow, steady, gradual change in the
ancestor as we collect it in progressively higher rocks.
We also know there wasn't any sudden jump, or "salta-
tion," from one to the other, as the descendant species
had already been in existence (albeit living elsewhere)
for millions of years before it suddenly appears in sedimentary rocks of the midwest.

Such a pattern is easily explained as a typical case
of speciation. The ancestral species divided, with most
of its members persisting unchanged over most of its
habitat. A few members became a new, slightly modified daughter species and remained geographically isolated for a long period of time—a classic case of
what the Victorians called "vicariance." What is surprising is merely the extreme conservatism these species, and most others of the fossil record, typically
exhibit. Once a species has evolved and become established, it is not unusual to find that it persisted virtually unchanged for an additional five or ten million
years—and sometimes even longer. New species arise
rather rapidly and do not seem to be the outcome of
a long, slow, progressive modification of the ancestor.
This is the basis of the notion of "punctuated equilibria"—that long intervals of nonchange ("stasis") last
for far greater periods of time than the brief intervals of
a few thousand years it takes to produce a new species.

The idea of "punctuated equilibria" does not directly attack the notion of natural selection—or, for that matter, any other aspect of genetic theory. What it does attack is the straightforward *extrapolation* of natural selection that sees adaptive modification of a species over a period as long as, say, a million years, as inevitable. The flip-side of the notion that evolution is slow, steady, and progressive, requiring millions of years, is that, given a million years, change is inevitable. The fossil record strongly suggests, however, that although change *can* be slow, it is more frequently episodic and can occur in but a few thousands of years. And, given a million years, if it survives at all, a species will tend to persist with little or no change. Given a change in its environment, a species will be more likely to move out or to become extinct, rather than undergo the kind of transformation necessary to enable it to continue living there.

But there *is* an anomaly here. For although good examples of slow, progressive change from an ancestor into its descendant are few and far between, nonetheless the fossil record is full of examples of progressive change. Horses, to take but one, got larger, lost the side toes on their feet, and evolved progressively larger and more complicated teeth (for grazing). Our own lineage shows progressive increase in both absolute body size and relative brain size. Yet, *within* individual fossil species in both the horse and human lineages, there is little evidence of gradual progressive change of the sort we would expect from the operation of pure natural selection. What we see, again, is persistence of species once they appear—and persistence in a virtually unchanged condition. There is, instead, a pattern of differential *species* survival underlying the directional patterns of change we frequently do observe in the fossil record. Over the past four million years, brain size has increased within our lineage. But each of the fossil hominid species, once evolved, retained its original brain size. From time to time, new species with bigger brains evolved, and over the years less brainy species have dropped by the wayside, while the brainier ones survived. This, the sort of interpretive scenario called "species selection," is one outcome of paleontological observations of the past decade. It is part of the controversy. As an idea, it may or may not be right. It is a return to the more pluralistic view originally espoused by Charles Darwin: Some paleontologists see selection between species as just as important as selection among individuals within species—the more narrow concept of natural selection held by twentieth-century genetics. Paleontologists were forced into this view because the kind of change one would expect to find in the fossil record—if all change were simply a smooth function of pure natural selection—simply is not there.

Note that just as in the case of nondarwinian evolution, this controversy is firmly within the context of the notion that life has evolved. What is at issue is the relative strength and intensities of the various forces that have produced the evolutionary patterns we see in nature. And if the supreme importance of the narrow form of natural selection is questioned by some paleontologists, they do not deny that natural selection plays an important role in the adaptive modification of species. Indeed, paleontologists are in no position to criticize natural selection in any detail—simply because there are too many gaps in the fossil record to study differential reproductive success generation by generation. Paleontologists can only consider the naïve extrapolation of natural selection through millions of years—and it must be admitted that most of the naïveté has come from the paleontologists. Paleontologists are now simply suggesting that more than one level of selection plays a role in shaping evolutionary patterns, and that the evolutionary process might be a wee bit more complicated than the modern synthesis saw it to be.

(3) Is Natural Selection Meaningless?

It is also fashionable these days to attack natural selection as a "tautology." Tautologies are simply definitions, but the word is frequently used pejoratively to mean "you haven't really said anything." If, for example, natural selection is defined as "survival of the fittest," and we ask "who are the fittest?" and we answer "those who survive," we have a tautology on our hands. But if we define natural selection as the process of differential reproductive success and we assert that, statistically speaking, it is those organisms best equipped to cope with the rigors of their environment (i.e., the "fittest") who are more successful in a world of finite resources, we again have a tautology. But we can theoretically set up experiments in the lab and in the wild and predict that organisms with certain features will outsurvive and outbreed those less well suited to whatever the prevailing conditions are. So natural selection can be predictive and, in any case, it is undeniable that there *is* a nonrandom process of differential reproductive success: true natural selection. But the problem with natural selection is that it is a concept developed to explain generation-by-generation change in gene frequencies within a population—and many evolutionary biologists, especially systematists and paleontologists, simply do not have that kind of data at their disposal. It has been frustrating for paleontologists to be told that the only known mechanism of any real importance in evolution is natural selection—and to realize that, strictly speaking, paleontologists can never study natural selection directly. Natural selection is useful as a directly testable scientific concept only on small-scale patterns of evolutionary change—and much of the controversy in evolutionary biology these days reflects this situation.

When all the dust settles from this latest episode of controversy in evolutionary theory, we will have a more accurate view of just how the evolutionary process works. That's the whole idea and what the game is all about. If evolutionary theory emerges in a somewhat altered form from the "modern synthesis," some of us will feel victorious, and others will go to their graves in unyielding opposition. If the synthesis escapes unscathed, some of us will have tried in vain, but the theory will be all the stronger from its ability to withstand severe criticism. It is the marketplace of ideas, and competition is keen. But this much is abundantly obvious: whatever emerges in the next ten years, it will only be a progress report. It is in the nature of things that nothing in science can possibly be the last word. We are truth-seekers, yes, but no one has yet invented a way of determining what the truth is when we have it. We merely stick to ideas as long as they seem to work. It is a mild understatement, at the very least, to point out that creationists don't feel this way about their ideas. Scratch a creationist and you find someone who knows in his bones he has the truth.

Chapter 5

CREATIONISTS ATTACK:
I. SCIENTIFIC STYLE AND NOTIONS OF TIME

GARNER TED ARMSTRONG, THAT HANDSOME AND AR-
ticulate electronic preacher, occasionally devotes one of
his shows to evolution. A few years ago I was idly
cruising the tv channels and came upon Armstrong's
gentle but firm rejection of evolution as a plausible explanation of nature's beauty and complexity. Up on the
screen popped a film clip showing thousands of silvery
grunions—small Pacific-coast fish—flopping around on
the beach in Santa Barbara in the moonlight. The
grunions were engaged in their annual reproductive
rites. Such unusual and complex behavior! marveled
Armstrong. Only a Creator, an Almighty God, could
have fashioned a fish with such a remarkably intricate
reproductive style.

Having gotten the message, I moved the channel
selector four spaces and found an episode of Jacob
Bronowski's "Ascent of Man" series on the educational
network. Lo and behold, Bronowski was in the throes
of his segment on evolution and I was treated to my
second view of Santa Barbara grunions within five
minutes. But what a difference in the moral! How
marvelous the process of evolution must be, mused
Bronowski, to produce such an intricate pattern of be-

havior in this little fish! The unwitting grunions had become a foil for each of the two dominant, competing explanations of "how life has come to be as we see it today." Both were frank appeals to the viewer's credulity; both asked us to ask ourselves: What do *I* believe? I decided to skip the whole thing and watch a movie.

But the coincidental Armstrong/Bronowski "debate" does highlight the basic premise of all recent creationist efforts to speak of "creation-science" or "scientific creationism." For creation-science isn't science at all, nor have creation scientists managed to come up with even a single intellectually compelling, scientifically testable statement about the natural world. At least ninety-five percent of all of their reams of privately published books and pamphlets are devoted to an attack on conventional science—the prevailing ideas of astronomy, geology, biology, and anthropology. Creationists acknowledge that their "science" consists mostly of such attacks; creation-science has precious few ideas of its own, *positive* ideas that stand on their own, independent of, and opposed to, counteropinions of normal science. And as we shall see, what few ideas there are that can be construed as scientific are fatuous.

Creationists get away with calling their work science by resorting to a simple trick: *if,* they say, there are only two possible ways something might happen, and *if* both are difficult to prove, *then* an equally viable approach is to disprove one—in which case its alternative is automatically proven. Since creationists admit the activities of a Creator cannot, by their very nature, be proven directly (but must instead be taken on faith), an attack on the credibility of evolution is the only logical way for them to proceed. And indeed this is how they do proceed. Those intrepid souls who have accepted creationist challenges to public debates have had a difficult time getting creationists to discuss religion, or the "creation-science model"—all creationists want to discuss is the credibility of scientific opinion on the age of the universe and of the earth and the manner of appearance of life's diversity.

Such a ploy has been effective, but not because of any inherent logic involved. After all, evolution and creationism are *not* strict alternatives. The scientific creationism that I am discussing here is a relatively new and rather virulent form of creationism. It is found in most of the recent creationist literature and forms the basis of the bills passed (as of this writing) by the legislatures and signed into law by the governors of Arkansas and Louisiana. And it is extreme. It insists that the earth and all of its life were created in six twenty-four-hour days by the act of a supernatural Creator. The inventors and exponents of scientific creationism seem to loathe "theistic evolution" (as they call it), at least as deeply as pure evolutionary biology and historical geology. Prominent creationist authors such as Henry Morris, Duane Gish, and R. L. Wysong are continually demonstrating the (to them) fallacy of the idea that God created the universe, the earth, and all life but did so using the natural laws of His universe. According to this line of thought, the six days of Genesis can be taken metaphorically and interpreted not as six literal twenty-four-hour days, but as vast periods, each of unspecified duration. *This* is the general way most theologians and lay religious persons have reconciled their faith with the findings of science over the past 150 years or so. *This* is the general position that most religious scientists (and there are many of them) adopt when considering how their work and their religious faith might be reconciled. The extreme creationists reject this approach, this so-called theistic evolution. They also airily dismiss all other religious explanations of "origins" and decide that the sort of conflict artificially created when the grunions are accidentally opposed on the airwaves one night is a *real* intellectual problem. The creationist claim, that an attack on evolution constitutes an automatic validation of creationism works only if we fall into their trap and accept at face value such either/or, black-and-white contrasts. Evolution-science and creation-science are antithetical only in the minds of this fervent few.

We have already seen that evolutionary biology is as scientific as, say, quantum mechanics. It makes predictions about what we should find in nature, and it is self-correcting. It never claims to have the final truth. It bears repeating here that creation-science, by its fundamental nature, *cannot* be construed as science: the essence of the hardline creationist position is that a supernatural Creator, using laws *no longer operating,* created the earth as we find it today. The members of the Creation Research Society, one of the major organizations devoted to the pursuit of scientific creationism, all hold advanced degrees in science or technology. And all are required to sign a pledge before admission to the Society: "The Bible is the written word of God, and because we believe it to be inspired thruout [*sic*], all of its assertions are historically and scientifically true in all of the original autographs. To the student of nature, this means that the account of origins in Genesis is a factual presentation of historical truth." Thus the truth is known at the outset, sworn in affidavit form. A supernatural Creator, using laws no longer in existence and therefore utterly beyond the purview of science to begin with, lies at the very heart of their credo. These are the "scientists," and this is their "science" that they want to inject into the science curricula of every school in the nation. If there is one rule, one criterion that makes an idea scientific, it is that it *must* invoke naturalistic explanations for phenomena, and those explanations must be testable solely by the criteria of our five senses. When creationists admit that their system invokes the supernatural, as they do even in Arkansas Statute 590 (which defines creation-science in part as "the scientific evidence and related inferences that indicate [1] sudden creation of the uni-

verse, energy and life from nothing"), they admit that
they are not doing science.

The literature of scientific creationism is not overly
large. The Creation Research Society has since 1964
published a journal, the *Creation Research Society
Quarterly*. A relatively small number of creation scientists have produced the vast bulk of the articles and
books that have appeared. None of them has contrib-
uted a single article to any reputable scientific journal.
The usual creationist retort to this last observation is
that conventional science scorns and ridicules creationism but inwardly fears it and thus refuses to publish creationist contributions—a charge not unlike that leveled
by otherwise serious people when Immanuel Velikovsky's ideas were being attacked by prominent scientists.
Creationists would love to inherit Velikovsky's mantle
of martyrdom. But anyone familiar with the scientific
literature of the past twenty years knows full well that
all manner of new, heretical—and sometimes rather
bizarre—ideas have been mooted in the pages of many
journals. Editors of such outlets are understandably
skeptical, but in the competitive marketplace that *is* the
scientific world, there is no problem getting an idea
published if it has the least semblance of merit. Indeed,
heresy is cherished in some quarters—if it is compelling heresy. There is no evidence that any creation
scientist has ever bothered to submit a manuscript to a
reputable scientific journal.

When looking at what the scientific creationists say,
then, we know it comes from privately published
sources and has not gone through the gauntlet of critical peer review. Religion permeates all but some of
the very latest scientific creationist books—and even
here it is only the "public school edition" that omits
the fundamentalist Christian connection underlying the
entire creationist effort. A few other elements emerge
as well. The literature is all written in extremely simple
terms, to convince the uninitiated rather than to enter
into a sophisticated dialogue with science. Moreover,

creationists are sloppy: they make simple spelling errors when quoting scientists. And they distort: creationists often go beyond mere quoting out of context and actually impute words and thoughts to scientists that are absent in the original version. Creationists are internally inconsistent—sometimes in incredible ways, as when they explain the fossil record and the existence of sedimentary rocks as the product of a single Noachian deluge, and then turn around and, accepting fossils as evidence of the existence of species over long periods of time (i.e., *not* the products of a single, brief episode of deposition from flood waters), use the sequence of fossils in the rocks to "disprove" evolution. They cite scientists with approbation if it serves their purpose, and reject the same scientists when it doesn't. Examples of all these will appear as we take a closer look at what the scientific creationists are actually saying these days.

What Are They Really Saying?

Creationists say a lot of things. When debating creationists, scientists are bombarded by a number of challenges creationists cull from scientific writings on the natural world. The argument takes the form: "All right, let's see you explain *this* one!" Hurling challenge after challenge, jumping from atomic physics to zoology, creationists eventually wear the opposition down with their compendia of nature's enigmas. One of their favorites, for example, is the bombardier beetle, darling of creationists because its intricate defense system (bombardier beetles forcefully eject hot fluids when threatened) is impossible (for creationists) to imagine evolving through a series of less perfect, intermediate stages—and, they say, impossible for an evolutionist to "prove." Some intrepid evolutionists take them up point by point, and there was a lively exchange on the bombardier beetle in the Summer 1981 issue of *Cre-*

ation/Evolution, a journal devoted to combatting the
creationist effort.

But such compendia of cases quickly become te-
dious, and in the end demonstrate nothing. Evolutionists
admit at the outset that they are puzzled by some of
nature's products, and, in any case, as scientists they
are in no position to "prove" anything. But there *are*
some general themes recurrent in the literature of scientific creationism—both general objections to "evolution
science," accompanied by countless examples, *and* a
body of statements that make up the corpus of creationist thought on "how things have come to be as
they are." The bombardier beetle, for example, is but
one of the many cases of the general argument that
intermediate stages between an anatomical structure
and its supposed precursor are impossible, could not
be produced by natural selection, and do not, in any
event, show up in the fossil record—once again, the
hydra-headed problem of "gaps." Other general objections include the argument that apparent design in
nature is a *prima facie* case for a Designer; that complex molecules, anatomical structures and behaviors
(cf. the grunions) "cannot have arisen by chance," the
probabilities of a natural process forming them being
remote; and that the evolution of the complex from the
simple violates more fundamental scientific laws—particularly the First and Second Laws of Thermodynamics, which, say creationists, enjoin the natural origin
of something out of nothing (the First Law) and man-
date that, once begun, a system inevitably declines and
cannot become more complex (the Second Law).
These and other sorts of objections, with their myriad
examples, are interwoven with various direct pronouncements to form the "creation-science" model.

Though it would be relatively simple to compile a
scientific creationist model from the various books and
pamphlets from such creationist authors as Morris,
Gish, Wysong, Gary Parker, and the few additional

creation scientists around, the scientific creation model given by lawyer Wendell R. Bird of the Institute for Creation Research (ICR) in the December, 1978 *Acts and Facts* (published by the Institute) is perhaps the best place to start. Bird's list of seven points succinctly summarizes the scientific creationist position and can serve as a springboard for discussing all the major creationist claims. In addition, it is the basis of the version of scientific creationism defined in Arkansas Statute 590—the "equal time" bill enacted in March, 1981.

Bird's scientific creation model is as follows: "(1) Special creation of the universe and earth (by a Creator), on the basis of scientific evidence. (2) Application of the entropy law to produce deterioration in the earth and life, on the basis of scientific evidence. (3) Special creation of life (by a Creator), on the basis of scientific evidence. (4) Fixity of original plant and animal kinds, on the basis of scientific evidence. (5) Distinct ancestry of man and apes, on the basis of scientific evidence. (6) Explanation of much of the earth's geology by a worldwide deluge, on the basis of scientific evidence. (7) Relatively recent origin of the earth and living kinds (in comparison with several billion years), on the basis of scientific evidence."

Arkansas Statute 590 defines creation-science:

(It) means the scientific evidence for creation and inferences from those scientific evidences. Creation-science includes the scientific evidences and related inferences that indicate: (1) Sudden creation of the universe, energy and life from nothing. (2) The insufficiency of mutation and natural selection in bringing about development of all living kinds from a single organism. (3) Changes only within fixed limits of originally created kinds of plants and animals. (4) Separate ancestry for man and apes. (5) Explanation of the earth's geology by catastrophism, including the occurrence of a worldwide flood. (6) A relatively recent inception of the earth and living kinds.

Quick comparison shows Bird's model and the definition of creation-science in the Arkansas law to be virtually identical. The law merely combines Bird's first and third points into one statement ([1] of the statute), and substitutes a statement about the insufficiency of mutation and natural selection to produce life's diversity for Bird's harping on the Second Law of Thermodynamics as its second point. All the rest is the same—even the order. Thus Bird's statement of the scientific creationist position is especially important because it has served as the basis for legislation. It is the form the creationists have succeeded in getting passed in Arkansas. It contains the elements of what they wish to be added to the science curricula of all secondary schools in the United States.

Creationists as Theoretical Physicists

In *Evolution: The Fossils Say No!* (page 24), Duane Gish (associate director of the ICR and professor of natural science, Christian Heritage College) laments: "The reason that most scientists accept evolution is that they prefer to believe a materialistic, naturalistic explanation for the origin of all living things." He's right, of course—because scientists are constrained to frame *all* their statements in "naturalistic" terms simply to be able to test them. When a scientific-creation model such as Bird's, or the definition of such a model enacted as a state law, avers that the origins of the universe, the earth, and life were the acts of a Creator, they are *automatically* excluding such a model from the realm of science. (The law changes Bird's "Creator" to "creation"—but "creation," especially "from nothing," must directly imply a Creator, as all the creationist literature openly admits.) Gish (*op. cit.*, p. 40) has admitted that "We do not know how the Creator created, what processes He used, *for He used processes which are not now operating anywhere in the natural universe* [italics in original]. This is why we refer to creation as special creation. We cannot discover by scientific investigations anything about the creative processes used by the Creator." Taking Alexander Pope's injunction "presume not God to scan; the proper study of Mankind is Man" to its literal extreme, creationists admit at the outset that creationism in any guise really isn't science at all. One would think that this alone would be enough to keep creationism out of the science curricula of schools. It's simply a matter of definition—of what is science and what is not. By its very definition, scientific creationism cannot be science.

Creation of something from nothing, creationists say, is supernatural. "Matter can be neither created nor destroyed" is the popular cant rendition of the First Law of Thermodynamics. Creationists like Morris say "evolutionists" (meaning, simply, "scientists") cheat when they admit they don't know how the universe started. Whence all those particles of matter? Creationists deride the "who knows—maybe it was always there" shrug of an answer most scientists give. The ultimate origin of matter, beyond any specific theory of a "big bang" origin of the universe and development of the various kinds of atoms, molecules, stars and galaxies, really *is* a mystery that no scientist honestly can claim to have much insight about. Scientists admit it when they don't have the faintest idea why or how something happened—and the ultimate origin of matter is a beautiful example. But the creationists *know*.

The Second Law of Thermodynamics—that all systems tend toward decay and disorder (increase in entropy)—is a great favorite of scientific creationism. Claiming that the Creator first created the earth and all its life, *then* set the First and Second Laws into motion, creationists see the "law of inevitable decline" as *the* fatal objection to evolution. Evolution is the development of the complex from the simple, they say, precisely the opposite of what you would predict from the Second Law. Morris, in *The Scientific Case for Creation* (Morris directs the ICR), has a graph (p. 6) showing the creationist expectation: after a perfect beginning, things have gone downhill on earth—the Second Law working in its inexorable fashion.

Morris dismisses an apparent exception to the Second Law: at the moment of fertilization, a human egg is a single, microscopic cell. That cell divides; its daughter cells divide, and so on. The adult human consists of billions of cells. But we are not gigantic multi-celled eggs. During development, cells differentiate and take on different forms. They are grouped into specialized tissues, and these into organs. Creationists admit that adults are, in a basic sense, more complex than the eggs from which they sprung—though each cell has the same nature and amount of genetic information in its DNA as contained in the original fertilized egg. But the process of development from egg to adult does not violate the Second Law of Thermodynamics because it is only temporary. Death is inevitable, and with it, decay. The Second Law triumphs in the end.

And, biologists point out, so it will in evolution. It is as certain as anything in science that the sun will not last forever. If, in another fifteen billion years, it becomes a red giant in its dying days, the earth will be consumed. In any event, burn out the sun and the source of our energy is gone. Life will, inevitably, cease to exist. The law will win out. Anyone who has taken a college course in paleontology knows that the vast majority of species that ever lived are already extinct. Some species appear to last for millions of years, but the overwhelming conclusion from the fossil record is that no species can last forever, regardless of what eventually happens to the sun. So, the Second Law is working here, too.

But all this is, in a very real sense, merely playing with words, the way the creationists do. Yes, all systems will run down—if there is no fresh input of energy into them. Plants trap only a fraction of the sun's energy that comes our way; the energy is trapped in the form of sugars, which form the base of the food chain sustaining all animal life. The atmosphere, oceans, and rocky surface of the earth's crust retain some solar energy in the form of heat. All the rest is reflected back out to space (with a minute amount bounced back again from the moon and artificial satellites). The system isn't running down—it is, instead, "open" with this continual influx of solar energy. Life uses only a fraction of this available energy: there is far more available than is actually used. Faced with this argument, Morris and colleagues have rewritten the Second Law, not with the language of mathematics appropriate to the task (were they scientists), but with simple English. Faced with the objection that the Second Law applies only to "closed" systems, creationists have simply changed the Second Law—first claiming, that it applies to all systems, and then speaking about a system requiring an "energy conversion mechanism" and a "directing program." In the words of Stanley Freske (writing in *Creation/Evolution*, Spring 1981, p. 10): "Creationists are not showing that evolution contradicts the second law of thermodynamics; instead, they are saying that the second law, as accepted by conventional science, is incorrect and insufficient to explain natural phenomena. They insist that something else of their own making must be added—namely a divinely created directing program or a distinction between different kinds of entropy." Freske refers to this creationist revision of the Second Law as the "creative Trinity." Creationists' use of the Second Law as a general falsification of evolution is a wonderful example of bad science, and (because at first they didn't realize that the law applies only to closed systems) of desperate attempts to salvage their notion. There is nothing about this that smacks of the scientific; it is, rather, the all-too-human attempt to preserve a pet idea at all costs—

even if it requires bending the rules of normal science to serve one's own ends.

Of Time and the Navel

Creationists say the universe, the earth, and all of life are young. All were created within the last few thousand years or so. Morris, Wysong, and other creationist apologists have devoted many pages to attacking the notion that the universe, earth, and life are billions of years old. And they have assembled "scientific evidence" purporting to show that the earth is only a few thousand years old. It is when they confront the rock record that scientific creationists have most vehemently attacked the integrity and judgment of scientists. In their discussions of historical geology, creationists have more than amply demonstrated their capacity for cleverly distorted "scholarship." And it is in their efforts to propound an alternative explanation for the observations of geologists that creationists reveal themselves for the pseudoscientists they really are.

The notion that the earth has had a truly long history is one of the great intellectual achievements of human thought. Though there had been occasional flashes of insight throughout history, there was no real *need* to consider the possibility that the world was vastly older than popularly imagined until the late-eighteenth and early-ninteenth centuries, when a few men began patiently examining the intricacies of the great sequences of rock strata in Europe. The Greek traveler and historian, Herodotus, remarked on the seashells he found on Mediterranean hillsides around 400 B.C. Many centuries later, Leonardo da Vinci understood the fossilized shark teeth he found in the surrounding Italian hills to be exactly what they *appeared* to be: the remains of ancient sharks inhabiting a sea of long ago. But the common conception of fossils up through Renaissance times saw them as petrified thunderbolts—or the work of the devil who put fossils in the earth to mislead us all. Today, according to ICR director Henry Morris, Satan's role is still perceived in this vein, as it is no less than the devil himself underlying the "well-nigh universal insistence that all this must have come about by evolution." (*The Twilight of Evolution,* p. 77)

Creationists accept fossils for what they are: dead remains of once-living organisms. Creationists believe dinosaurs existed, though some think they were wiped out in Noah's Flood, while others contend that Noah had some dinosaur couples on the Ark. In other words, fossils are real all right, but they simply aren't as old as evolutionists insist they are.

When confronted with the evidence that the universe, earth, and life really are vastly older than they would like to believe, creationists admit that things certainly *look* old. But, they say, this appearance of old age is illusory. Instead of blaming the devil for tricking us by making the earth and its living inhabitants seem old—the explanation preferred by their intellectual forebears in the Middle Ages—they blame . . . the Creator! When the Creator created all things, He created them to look as if they really did have a long history. He had to, creationists assert, simply because the universe had to be set in motion: light from distant stars had to have reached earth by the end of the sixth day, and rivers had to be already running in their courses. In short, the system had to be up and running at the very moment of creation. But light from distant stars, and streams running in their channels, look as if they've been there awhile. It takes time for light to travel interstellar distances or for streams to carve their channels. Creationists say the Creator's design included an instant history for the universe, earth, and life; after Creation, natural processes (such as the Laws of Thermodynamics) were set in motion, and light continues to reach us from distant heavenly sources, and streams continue to carve their channels.

When Darwin first published *The Origin* in 1859, he

disturbed a number of people. One of these was Philip Gosse, a clergyman who responded with a book of his own, which he called *Omphalos,* the ancient Greek word for "navel." Gosse developed an elaborate argument that it was God's intention to give the earth a semblance of history—just as he gave Adam a navel, even though Adam was not born of a woman.

Gosse included fossils in his catalogue of items God created to make us think the earth and life are truly old. Many of Gosse's fellow clergymen reacted in horror to this picture of a deceitful God. Little better than a nasty devil playing tricks on us, it seemed incomprehensible to most rational minds that a Creator-God would endow mankind with the ability to think—and at the same time take such elaborate steps to fool us. When scientific creationists today claim the Creator's efforts automatically established an apparent history, they are reverting to Gosse's *omphalos* argument—though of course they deny the Creator made this mere semblance of history simply to fool us. It is simply the way He had to do it. Either way, it doesn't make a great deal of sense.

What are the overwhelming evidences that the universe, earth, and life are vastly older than the six thousand years Archbishop Ussher computed from the pages of Genesis? The first inklings came when the Danish physician Niels Stensen—who wrote in Latin and used the Latinized version of his name, Nicolaus Steno—made a few commonsensical generalizations about sedimentary rocks in the mid-seventeenth century. Steno saw that most of the layered rocks of the earth's crust are formed of minute grains of sand, clay, lime, and other mineral substances. He knew that streams carried such particles and discharged them into lakes and seas and that such particles could be seen accumulating in such places today. From these elementary observations, Steno framed the Law of Superposition: sedimentary beds accumulate from the deposition of particles; the lower beds form first, the upper beds being piled on later on top of the lower beds. Thus, beds lying above other beds must be younger than the lower beds.

Creationists do not wholly dispute Steno's law in principle—though their thesis that all of the miles of thick sediments were formed during the forty-day Noachian deluge amounts to a rejection of Steno's simple proposition. Nor do creationists deny that some rocks are metamorphosed (altered by heat and pressure into crystalline form), while others are igneous, cooled from a molten mass such as volcanic lavas. But what they do reject is the complex chain of observation and reasoning begun in the late eighteenth century and based on the start given by Nicolaus Steno.

The physican and farmer, James Hutton, as we have already noted, essentially founded the modern science of geology when he methodically applied observation, common sense, and a knowledge of present-day processes to explain how the physical features of his Scottish landscape might have formed. Hutton was a "Plutonist"—he believed that some rocks, such as the lava flow forming "King Arthur's Seat" at Edinburgh, had cooled from a once-molten mass. His opponents were "Neptunists"—believing that *all* rocks, including granites and lavas, schists and sediments, had all precipitated out of an ocean that had encircled the globe in primordial times. *That* controversy died in the first half of the nineteenth century when it was conclusively shown that some rocks *must* have cooled from a molten state and that some igneous rocks (particularly lava flows) lay *above* older sediments. Neptunism, as an explanation for the formation of the sequence of rocks in the earth's crust, is the geologic equivalent of pangenesis, the theory of inheritance adopted by Darwin and other nineteenth-century biologists. Both are now thoroughly outmoded.

But Hutton prompted another controversy, one that the scientific creationists claim is still alive. Hutton used observations of what was going on in nature around

him in the present to interpret the events of the past—
just as Steno, da Vinci, and Herodotus did before him.
A conflict soon arose: Huttonian geologists saw the
action of wind and rain eroding rocks and sending
particles rushing downstream to be deposited as an open
vista of long periods of gradual change. Their opponents, such as the French scientist Baron Cuvier and the
English clergyman William Buckland, saw it otherwise:
called catastrophists, they interpreted geological history
as a series of sudden, even violent, happenings, inter-
spersed with periods of quiescence. Cuvier thought
that the fossil record of life revealed not one, but an
entire series of separate creations. Buckland saw the
physical history of the earth as a series of cataclysmic
events—the last one being the Great Flood of Genesis.
Modern creationists, of course, reject these rather complex notions of catastrophism, calling merely for creation of the world and all living "kinds," *then* cata-
strophic flood, and *then* the resultant configuration of
things more or less as we see them today. Creationists
see themselves as "neo-catastrophists"—and impugn
the evolutionists as "uniformitarians."

We owe the concept of uniformitarianism primarily
to the English geologist Charles Lyell, who followed
Hutton's lead and developed a truly coherent science
of geology. Lyell, who was to prove so influential on
Darwin, yet who rejected evolution until his later years,
spoke of the uniformity of geological processes in his
famous *Principles of Geology,* published in the years
1830–33. Creationists today, presumably out of simple
ignorance, have utterly misconstrued the modern understanding of Lyell's uniformitarianism. As Stephen Jay
Gould and others have pointed out, uniformitarianism
meant at least two things to nineteenth-century geologists. It meant that we can seek to understand events
of the earth's past by studying processes of change still
going on today. It also implied that slow processes,
such as the erosion and deposition of sediments, further indicated that all events in earth history occurred

at uniform, and usually rather slow, rates. According to this second meaning of uniformitarianism—i.e., "gradualism"—great changes are the result strictly of the gradual accumulation of minute changes over formidably long periods of time.

The first of these ideas attached to the word "uniformitarianism" is simply common sense—and a cardinal assumption if we are to do science at all. The laws of nature we see operating today were operative in the past as well, unless there is reason to suspect otherwise. In other words, water has run downhill and the earth has revolved around the sun ever since there has been an earth, water, and hills. This is merely the naturalistic assumption, the requirement that all scientific explanations must be couched in terms of processes we have reason to believe are operating in nature—a notion totally counter to the creationist position that different rules were in force at the time of Creation, and processes we see operating today were invented by the Creator only after He had created. This first meaning of uniformitarianism is simply another way of stating how all of science is done.

The *other* meaning of uniformitarianism, however, is another kettle of fish entirely. When creationists say (as they do in Arkansas Statute 590) that *they* are catastrophists, while "evolution-scientists" are uniformitarians, they mean that they believe that events of the past were often, if not always, sudden, violent, and cataclysmic. They have the Flood specifically in mind, of course. But geologists long ago abandoned this second meaning of uniformitarianism—that all changes in earth history were the product of infinitesimally minute changes gradually accumulating through time. For well over a century now, we have spoken of the Ice Ages in the recent geological past, when four times huge ice fields have grown over the continents of the Northern Hemisphere. There is similar evidence for glaciers, not throughout all geologic history, but at different points of time in the past—for example, in the Southern

Hemisphere 240 million years ago. Volcanoes and earthquakes are truly sudden in their action, and many wreak huge changes. And the recent invocation of an asteroid impact as the trigger to the ecological collapse that ended the Cretaceous world and wiped out perhaps as many as ninety percent of all living species is a catastrophe *par excellence* (and even if there was no asteroid, the extinction "event" itself was a disaster). As we have seen, it is now becoming fashionable to view everything from the evolution of species to the mass extinctions and subsequent proliferations that pepper life's history as a sequence of episodic change—not the slow, steady, gradual change this second meaning of uniformitarianism implies. No, indeed, creationists cannot justifiably claim that they, and they alone, recognize that events in the history of the earth and its life frequently reflect episodic events rather than slow, steady, progressive change—as Wendell Bird and the Arkansas legislature would have it. Creationists do stand alone as "anti-uniformitarians" because only they are willing to suspend natural laws, as we think we understand them today, to frame an *ad hoc* explanation of the Creator's acts in bringing the universe, earth, and life into existence a few short thousands of years ago. But such a stance does not allow them to claim as their own the valid part of the old catastrophism—the notion that the nature of historical events is frequently more episodic than gradual.

The idea that the earth is a product of development through natural processes does imply a history. And documenting the history of a stream downcutting its channel over, say, a ten-year period, does automatically suggest that it must have taken quite a while for the Colorado River to cut through the ten thousand feet of rock of the Kaibab Plateau to form the Grand Canyon. By inference, it was beginning to look to nineteenth-century geologists like six thousand years was just not enough time for everything they were finding out about earth history to have happened.

One of the most important weapons in the creationist arsenal is the assertion that the entire scheme of earth history worked out by geologists is based on faulty logic, or circular reasoning. Henry Morris (p. 32 of *The Scientific Case for Creation*), for example, says: "Most people do not realize that the very existence of the long geological ages is based on the assumption of evolution." And (p. 35), "How can the fossil sequence prove evolution if the rocks containing the fossils have been dated by those fossils on the basis of the assumed stage of evolution of those same fossils? This is pure circular reasoning, based on the arbitrary assumption that the Evolution Model is true." This is the essence of the creationist attack on the notion of a truly old earth: how do geologists "tell time"? they ask, and then they tell you that, despite what you might think, most rocks cannot be dated directly by measuring the amount of radioactive decay of various atoms. (This is true.) Instead, they say, geologists use fossils to tell time: they arrange their fossils according to a supposed evolutionary sequence, they correlate rocks all over the world using this supposed sequence, and *then* they turn around and claim the fossil record *proves* evolution. Creationists have even maintained that when fossils are found out of the "proper" sequence, they are ignored—a charge which is nothing short of a vicious lie. If geologists and paleontologists really were as stupid and self-deceiving as creationists claim, their activities *would* be as circular and worthless as creationists say they are. The crux of their argument is that the myth of the "geologic column" and time scale is upheld against all contrary evidence by geologists and paleontologists who wish to preserve evolution at all costs. This is a serious charge and is, of course, false.

The truth is that the geologic column—the thick sequence of strata containing the outlines of events in earth history, events that allow us to subdivide particularly the last half billion years—was worked out in the first half of the nineteenth century. Though still being refined today (science marches on, after all), the basic divisions of geologic time were established well before Darwin published *The Origin* in 1859. In fact, to the extent that they held any publicly expressed opinions on the subject at all, the geologists who established the basic sequence of divisions of geologic time back then were creationists. The charge that the sequence of subdivisions of geologic time—with the Paleozoic, Mesozoic, and Cenozoic Eras as the main divisions of the past six hundred million years—is a ploy to support the false doctrine of evolution, is simply untrue. Paleozoic, Mesozoic, and Cenozoic mean, respectively, "ancient, middle, and recent life," referring to the animals and plants fossilized in these rocks—whose sequence was worked out independently of any notion of evolution.

How was the geologic column really developed? Creationists point out the indisputable fact that no single place on earth—even in cases like the Grand Canyon, or in the thick sedimentary sequences exposed in such mountain chains as the Alps, Rockies, or Andes—has the full geologic column. Portions are always missing. In the 1820s and 1830s, Roderick Murchison and Adam Sedgwick set out to study the sequence of strata lying below the Old Red Sandstone in the British Isles. Using Steno's rule that lower rocks are older than those lying above them, Sedgwick studied the sequence of rocks in Wales from the bottom up. Murchison, meanwhile, working some distance away, was tracing a sequence of layers down. Murchison paid particular attention to the occurrence of fossils in the rocks, while Sedgwick concentrated more on the mineral content. Both men worked by documenting the physical position of the strata—i.e., which strata overlay which. Each worked out a sequence of position of the rock layers of their areas simply by careful observation. Murchison showed that his rocks underlay the Old Red Sandstone. Sedgwick showed he had the oldest rocks of the sequence in Wales, and worked his way up. Sedgwick called his rocks Cambrian, after Cambria, the Roman word for Wales. Murchison called his rocks Silurian, for the Silures, an ancient tribe of the region.

The two men, friends and colleagues at first, soon got into a bitter dispute. As Murchison kept tracing his sequence downward, while Sedgwick came up, they soon found themselves discussing the same rocks. Each claimed the intermediate rocks under dispute to belong to his sequence—an argument not resolved until 1879, when Charles Lapworth named all the rocks between Sedgwick's original Cambrian and Murchison's upper Silurian beds the "Ordovician" (after the Ordovices, yet another ancient tribe). Today we still recognize the Cambrian, Ordovician and Silurian as the three oldest subdivisions ("Periods") of the Paleozoic Era. Anyone can still go to southwestern England and Wales and examine the *physical sequence* of rocks that led to the definition of these three geological periods. It is the physical what-lies-on-what observations that provide the real basis for studying geologic time.

Now it is certainly true that we call some rocks in the United States and elsewhere around the world "Cambrian," "Ordovician," or "Silurian." And it is here that scientific analysis—the testing of hypotheses by seeing if predicted patterns actually occur in nature—comes into play. William Smith, a British surveyor, showed the way. Henry Morris calls Smith's technique "old" simply because it was invented 150 years ago (i.e., also prior to the general acceptance of any idea of evolution)—as if the age of an idea has anything to do with its validity. (On those grounds, it is time to get rid of the ideas that the earth is round and revolves around the sun). Smith was surveying the terrain for one of the ambitious canal projects brought on by the Industrial Revolution. Climbing the hills, he noted that the fossils he saw *always* occurred in the same order. He could stand on one hill and predict what he would find on the next, based on his experience with the order of fossils. He could predict, if someone showed him a suite of fossils, what fossils would be found below them, and what one could expect to find above them. He found he could take a mixed collection of fossils and tell the collector, correctly, what the sequence of fossils had been as they lay in the rocks.

There is no assumption of evolution here. It is simple observation: fossils occur in the same general sequence everywhere they are found. When pronouncing two bodies of rock strata—no matter how widely separated they may be—to be roughly equivalent in age ("correlative") on the basis of their fossils, there is no evolutionary presupposition whatsoever. The only assumption is that identical, or nearly identical, fossils are the remains of organisms that lived at roughly the same time all over the earth. This is the basis, for instance, for stating that rocks of Cambrian, Ordovician, and Silurian age occur in the United States as well as in Great Britain where they were originally studied. We have found Cambrian trilobites, Orodvician trilobites, and other fossils in the United States—called Cambrian because they are, in some instances, dead ringers for the British fossils. Moreover, these fossils in the United States occur *in the same basic sequence* as the ones Sedgwick and Murchison found early in the nineteenth century in the rocks of England and Wales. So the correlation of rocks—saying two bodies of rock are about the same age—is *not* based on the assumption that evolution has occurred. It is based on simple empirical observation of the order in which fossils occur in strata and on the standard procedures of scientific prediction and testing by further observation. And now we even have an independent means of cross-checking our assumption that similar fossils imply rough equivalence of age for the formation of two or more bodies of rock. For now we have radiometric dating as an independent check.

Geologists quickly saw the potential for the direct

chemical dating of rocks soon after Madame Curie discovered radioactivity. Creationists, of course, dispute the use of radioactive decay for the direct dating of rocks. They attack atomic physics, without the empirical data or the necessary mathematical treatment, when they claim that the fundamental assumption of radiometric dating is in error. For geochemists simply assert that unstable nuclei of some kinds of atoms (i.e., isotopes of some elements) emit radiation at statistically constant rates, and in so doing are transformed into another isotopic form. *If* we know the original amount of the "parent" and "daughter" isotopes at the time a rock was formed, and *if* we know the rate at which the parent isotope decays to its daughter isotopic form, we would be able to measure the current ratio of daughter to parent and thus calculate how long ago the rock was in its initial state. Aha! cry the creationists, lots of assumptions there! How do we know that decay rates are constant? Though some laboratory experiments showing that extremes of temperature and pressure fail to alter decay rates, it is true that we must make this assumption—just as we assume that gravity has always been in operation as we observe it today.

But just look at the results. We can take a sample of rock—say, a granite from Nova Scotia. We know it is Devonian because it intrudes rocks with what we call Devonian fossils, but is itself overlain by slightly younger sediments—as judged by the fossil content. Someone from a geochemical lab takes several samples and analyzes the age by three different decay paths between isotopes of uranium and lead. The ages all come out to be around 380 million years—with a small "plus or minus" error factor of a few million years. (A few million years sounds like a huge error, but a couple of million years one way or the other is a small error compared with the huge age calculated. Saying "380 million years plus or minus two million" is like thinking back to April from December, and saying you can't remember whether something happened on the 19th, 20th, or 21st.) Now, someone from another lab comes along, samples the same Nova Scotia granite, and gets the same results. Then someone else dates a different Devonian granite—one, say, from Greenland—also associated with Devonian fossils. Sure enough, it works. Rocks predicted to be nearly the same age on the basis of their fossil content always turn out to be nearly the same age when radiometric dates are obtained. And rocks predicted to be older or younger than others always turn out to be older or younger—by the predicted number of millions of years—when dated radiometrically. In short, by now we have literally thousands of separate analyses using a wide variety of radiometric techniques. It is an interlocking, complex system of predictions and verified results—not a few crackpot samples with wildly varying results, as creationists would prefer to believe.

Creationists have catalogues of anomalous results from such dating procedures. None of these anomalies persist when samples are reanalyzed. Perhaps the most dramatic demonstration of the validity and accuracy of modern geologic dating comes from the deep-sea cores stored by the thousands in various oceanographic institutions. The direct sequence is preserved in these drill cores, of course, and the microscopic fossils in them allows the usual "this-is-older-than-that" sort of relative dating to be done. We can also trace the pattern of changes in the orientation of the earth's magnetic field: as you go up a core, portions are positively charged, while others are negative. Major magnetic events, reflecting a flipping of the earth's magnetic poles, are recognizable, and the sequence of fossils, the same from core to core, always matches up with the magnetic history in the same fashion from core to core. *Then,* when we obtain absolute dates from the cores (usually by using oxygen isotopes), we *always* find that the date of the base of the "Jaramillo event"—one of the pole-switching episodes—always yields a date of about 980,000 years ago. The dates are *always* the same (again, with a minor plus-or-minus factor). They are *always* in the right order. They are *always* in the tens or hundreds of thousands of years for the most recent dates, and in the millions of years further down the cores. There is such a complex system of cross-checking of independent ways of assessing age—all pointing to the same results—that I must remind myself that scientists cannot claim to have the ultimate truth. That the history of the deep-sea ocean basins as presently constituted goes back over one hundred million years is as close to certainty as the proposition that the earth is round.

We have as yet found no rocks directly dated at 4.5 billion years, the estimated age of the earth. This is James Hutton's original prediction, as he correctly surmised that the ravages of time preclude the survival of the most ancient crustal materials. The oldest rocks so far found are only about 3.8 billion years old. The oldest moon rocks, as well as stony meteorites, however, do yield dates of 4.5 billion years, agreeing well with the extrapolated age predicted by geochemists of 4.5 billion years for the age of the earth—a prediction made long before we sent someone to the moon to pick up some samples. No, it won't work. There are far too many independent lines of evidence—*none* of which is based on the assumption of, let alone an underlying commitment to, evolution—that amply confirm what geologists thought must be so 150 years ago: the earth simply cannot be a mere ten thousand years old. This is no story concocted by a Creator as part of His creative process. The earth really is incredibly old. And, of course, the universe is even older—fifteen billion years or so, an estimate based on the speed of light and the calculated distance between the center of the universe and its most remote objects. Appearances may be deceiving, of course. The Creator could be only making it look this way. But, leaving a Creator aside as science must, this is the mundane calculation of modern astronomers: fifteen billion years.

But the creationists do not give up. Morris has even written that even if the world were as old as geologists say, evolution still would not be proven—which, of course, is correct. But creationists do passionately care that the earth be proven to be young, and all the features of the geologic record be interpretable as essentially the product of one single event—Noah's Flood.

Creationists flatly accuse geologists of covering up the facts to preserve their pet theory of evolution. They point to "polystrate fossils" (their term)—by which they mean fossils (usually trees) that are standing vertically, and therefore must be sticking up through millions of years of time—if the "evolutionists" can be believed. Here they pretend that geologists insist that sedimentation rates must always be slow, steady and even—instead of the truly rapid rates that are sometimes observed. "Polystrate" trees show every sign of extremely rapid burial, generally when rivers flood over their banks.

But the creationists' favorite ploy to discredit the notion that there is an orderly sequence of rocks and fossils in the earth's crust lies in their distortion of large-scale rock displacement—so-called (by geologists) thrust faulting. Creationists point to large areas of the earth where the fossils seem to be out of sequence. And this is true: in many mountain belts, geologists sometimes find rocks that are younger in the sequence seen in over ninety-five percent of the places where such rocks are exposed, but overlain by rocks dated as older. Creationists say a convenient *ad hoc* explanation—one which they find incredible—is advanced to explain this "fatal flaw" of historical geology away: the concept of massive thrust faulting.

Creationists have been uncharacteristically silent so far on the notion of plate tectonics (earlier known as continental drift), where huge slabs of the earth's crust ("plates") are hypothesized to change their position with respect to one another over the course of geologic time. For example, peninsular India is reconstructed as part of the Southern Hemisphere supercontinent "Gondwana" for much of geologic time, breaking off only about seventy million years ago and eventually reaching Eurasia (about twenty million years ago), and in so doing buckling and thickening the crust and forming the Himalayas. Part of the enormous energy such processes involve has produced large-scale horizontal movements, where sections of the earth's crust have moved many miles laterally. (All true mountain belts are folded, like the pleats of an accordion, so that mountain belts are all more narrow now than they were as deep basins, when they were accumulating their huge sequences of sediments.)

Creationists pick examples—their favorite is the Lewis thrust in Montana, where Precambrian (one-billion-year-old) rocks lie on top of fossiliferous Cretaceous rocks only about ninety million years old. Evolution-scientists, we are told, invoke the ludicrous, unsupported notion of overthrusting simply to preserve their precious geologic sequence and the idea of evolution. And it is true that geologists mapping rocks, when they find Precambrian overlying Cretaceous rocks, suspect that something is amiss—because the *rest* of the world has the sequence the other way around. No two overthrust situations are alike: there is no general pattern of anomaly of Precambrian on Cretaceous. The next example may well be Cambrian on top of Devonian. Clearly, there are occasional anomalies in the record—but the anomalies themselves form no single coherent pattern.

Is it true that paleontologists invoke overthrusting to save their story? Are there no independent ways to demonstrate that massive dislocation of strata has occurred? Well, there are, and here is a good example of poor scholarship and out-and-out creationist chicanery: I have a creationist book (J. G. Read, *Fossils, Strata and Evolution*) devoted almost solely to the overthrust problem. In it the author says, in effect, that here is a real overthrust, and we can tell it is so because there is physical evidence (usually a zone of pulverized rock) between the two layers. When such massive crustal movement occurs, it must leave some direct effect on the rocks. Read doesn't tell us that the way his "real" examples of overthrusts were first detected was by the anomalous occurrence of fossils. The next step for Read and other creationists (such as Henry Morris) is to turn to what they consider "phony" examples, the truly massive cases such as the Lewis overthrust. Picture after picture (in Read's book) shows the Precambrian rocks sitting over Cretaceous shales—all without a trace, so they claim, of physical deformation. Do examples like the Lewis overthrust merely represent the last-ditch efforts of geologists to salvage the geologic column? Are there no independent means of demonstrating the reality of massive examples of overthrusting like the Lewis overthrust?

According to Christopher Weber, in a recent article in *Creation/Evolution,* the oft-repeated claim that there is no physical evidence of faulting between the Precambrian and underlying Cretaceous of the Lewis thrust is simply false. Weber writes:

Whitcomb and Morris [p. 187—*Genesis Flood,* 1961] lift the following words from this article [i.e., a professional geologic report by C. P. Ross and Richard Rezak, *The Rocks and Fossils of Glacier National Monument,* 1959]:

"Most visitors, especially those who stay on the roads, get the impression that the Belt strata (i.e., the Precambrian) are undisturbed and lie almost as flat today as they did when deposited in the sea which vanished so many million years ago."

But [Weber continues] if we read the rest of Ross' and Rezak's paragraph, we find that Whitcomb and Morris quoted it out of context:

". . . so many million years ago. Actually, they are folded, and in certain places, they are intensely so. From points on and near the trails in the park, it is possible to observe places where the Belt series, as revealed in outcrops on ridges, cliffs, and canyon walls, are folded and crumpled almost as intricately as the soft younger strata in the mountains south of the park and in the Great Plains adjoining the park to the east."

Even more damning is the thin layer of shale said to occur between the two rock units, evidence of thrusting (as crushed rock) in some areas, but evidence of tranquility (undeformed strata) in the case of the Lewis overthrust, as far as creationists are concerned. Such thrusting, less widespread than creationists would have us believe, and always confined to zones of mountain building where rocks are ordinarily highly disturbed, are not the *ad hoc* saviors of evolution. Like any other proposition in geology, overthrusts are based on physical evidence—though fossils out of sequence help geologists to spot overthrusts in the first place.

The Noachian Deluge and the Fossil Record

The one area where creation-scientists have made definitive statements—alternative explanations about how things have come to be as we find them today—rather than simple attacks on conventional science, lies in the use of a Great Flood to explain the occurrence of all sedimentary rocks and fossils over the face of the earth. Although the only research of which I am aware that this notion is said to have inspired was a couple of abortive "arkeological" expeditions to Mt. Ararat, nonetheless the creationist position can be examined on its own merits.

Charles Schuchert, an eminent geologist at Yale in the early twentieth century, published an *Atlas of Paleogeographic Maps* toward the end of his productive career. Thumbing through these maps, anyone can see that today we are in a relatively unusual period of earth history: the continents today are abnormally dry. The more usual condition by far is for the seas to be flooded over most of the continental interiors. Schuchert's maps reveal a kaleidoscopic pattern of flooding and emergence as the seas waxed and waned over the continents during the last half billion years. Why was the Silurian missing in southern Indiana, when creationist Gary Parker sallied forth looking for it in his college geology class? Actually, the Silurian is so well represented in southern Indiana that I doubt the example is valid, but there are places (such as the area just southwest of Albany, New York) where Devonian rocks sit directly on the Ordovician—and the Silurian is missing. Geologists explain such situations by saying that this area was emergent (dry land) during the Silurian; earlier, during the Ordovician and later, during parts of the Devonian, it was under the inland seas. And geologists agree with Parker that such widespread geological formations as the St. Peter Sandstone, which blankets much of the interior of the North American continent, bespeaks widespread flooding. But Parker and his cohorts want to explain the entire sedimentary record as the product of one single deluge a few thousand years ago—derived, perhaps, from a "vapor envelope" encircling the earth.

So here we have it—a sedimentary rock record, in some places tens of thousands of feet thick (as in the Andes) and in some other places totally absent (as over parts of central Canada, where erosion has removed what little amount of sediments ever did cover

the granitic core of the North American continent).
Geologists explain the uneven distribution of sediments, in other words, by normal processes of sediment
deposition and erosion: deposition where the seas
covered the land, erosion when the rocks of the crust
are exposed to the atmosphere. Scientific creationists
see the entire sequence as the result of one cataclysmic
deluge.

Here is the model creationists have picked up, with
little sign of comprehension: the geological notion of
facies. The "facies concept" points to the simultaneous
development of different environments and habitats in
different parts of the world. Walking from the seashore
inland on the eastern and western coasts of the United
States, for example, takes one from marine habitats, to
beaches, then perhaps to lagoons, then to marshes,
coastal forests, swamps, and mountains. If all were
preserved, each would look differently in the rock
record—and certainly the kinds of animals and plants
preserved as fossils would be different from habitat to
habitat.

So far, so good. Geologists have been aware of this
for years—different kinds of rocks, with utterly different fossil content, may nonetheless be contemporaneous because they were formed in different environments
that existed on earth at the same time. Creationists
claim that this ecological zonation will automatically
produce the general order of life paleontologists have
found in the fossil record: trilobites, brachiopods, and
other invertebrates should appear first—after all, they
were *already* living on the bottom of the sea. Simple,
spherical organisms will tend to sink faster than more
complex invertebrates, so we have "hydrodynamic
selectivity" in addition, to help put the simple creatures at the bottom of the sedimentary pile. Living
on land, amphibians, reptiles, birds, and mammals will
be buried later by the Flood—thus they will appear
higher up in the rock record, as the seas filled up and
encroached on the land. The more clever and advanced

the animal, the more successful one would predict it to
be (according to creationists, that is) in avoiding
calamity—so dinosaurs are found in lower beds than
mammals (actually, not by much!) and man appears
only in the uppermost layers of the sedimentary record.
That is their answer: ecological zonation, hydrodynamic selectivity, and relative success at fleeing to higher
elevations; three points of "explanation" of the sedimentary and fossil record according to the scientific-
creationist model of a single, worldwide Flood. Furthermore, since conditions would have been chaotic
during the Flood, naturally we would predict some
exceptions to the general sequence. This is the cream of
creationist pondering over how things have come to
be as we see them today.

Never mind that the record is, in places, tens of thousands of feet thick, with abundant evidence that much
of it (such as limestones and finely laminated shales)
must have formed exceedingly slowly. Never mind that
careful geologic mapping in Colorado and Wyoming
shows perfectly clearly how marine rocks—with clams,
snails, ammonites, mosasaurs, and other creatures of
the Cretaceous briny deep—grade *laterally* into terrestrial dinosaur-bearing beds in Montana. Here is true
ecological zonation: Cretaceous animals, both vertebrates and invertebrates, living side by side and *not*
piled on top of one another. Two hundred million
years earlier, Devonian fish occupying streams and
preserved in the present-day Catskill and Pocono
Mountains were contemporaneous with shellfish living
offshore in the marine waters of western New York
and Pennsylvania.

It simply will not work. Too many geologists have
climbed over those rocks and have seen how they
overlie one another. Geologists on the whole don't
care a fig about evolution—haven't in the past, and as
far as I can tell, still don't care much about it today.
What they passionately do care about is the history of
the earth, and of one thing they are certain: the earth

has *had* a history, a tremendously long and complex history. To disparage the work of geologists over the past two hundred years, to try instead to foist on the naïve the charade that there is no tremendous rock record and that the people who have strived so arduously to understand it are merely fools, is as cavalier an act as I have been sorry to witness. Creationists are the liars, freely slinging mud at all who cross their peculiarly myopic view of the natural world.

Chapter 6

CREATIONISTS ATTACK:
II. THE ORIGIN AND HISTORY OF LIFE

WHEN ASKED FOR AN EXAMPLE OF EVOLUTION IN AC-
tion, biologists typically bring up the case of *Biston
betularia,* the English peppered moth. This species
comes in two basic colors—a mottled white and a
black form. The mottled white form beautifully
matches the lichens on many English trees, while the
black-colored moths stand out against the background
and are easier targets for moth-hungry birds. When
pollution from the factories killed the lichens and the
trees reverted to the darker color of natural bark during the Industrial Revolution, all of a sudden it was
the white form that was conspicuous. Black moths soon
outnumbered white ones until comparatively recently,
when the crusade against air pollution has once again
tipped the scales back in the white variety's favor: the
lichens are back in force and now it is the black moths
whose life expectancy is the lower of the two. Here,
evolutionists assert, is adaptive evolution, natural selection monitoring environmental change. Those moths
best suited to prevailing conditions are, on the average,
more likely to survive and reproduce. Here is a beautiful case of small-scale evolution in action.

It comes as no surprise, then, to find these English

moths well represented in creationist literature, too. And it was only a minor departure from their usual course to see that, rather than trying to debunk the example, creationists such as Gary Parker and Duane Gish accept the moth story—but claim it favors the creation model. But I was not prepared to find creationists—particularly Parker and Gish, perhaps the two most eloquent creation "biologists"—actually accepting the moths as examples of small-scale evolution by natural selection. Modern creationists readily accept small-scale evolutionary change *and* the origin of new species from old: "Of course, if someone insists on defining evolution as 'a change in gene frequency,' then the fly example 'proves evolution.' But it also 'proves creation,' since varying the amounts of already existing genes is what creation is all about." (Parker, *Creation: The Facts of Life,* p. 83.) By the "fly example," Parker meant a case posed to him by an unnamed biologist, where reproductive isolation between populations of a single ancestral species had resulted in the appearance of several new species—an even more radical case of evolution than the shifting frequencies in coloration of the British moths.

Biologists are understandably amazed by such statements. Can creationists actually admit that evolution occurs and still stick to their creationist guns and *deny* that evolution has produced the great diversity of life? In a word—Yes! This is precisely what they do. The sorts of examples of evolution that biologists give, according to creationists, have nothing to do with the wholly new, the truly different. The creationist model is clear on this point: the Creator created basic "kinds," each kind replete with its own complement of genetic variation. Natural selection and reproductive isolation have worked on each "basic kind," sorting out this primordial variation to produce various specialized types. Creationist R. L. Wysong, a veterinarian, likens the process to the production of the panoply of dog breeds by artificial selection—the great array of different dogs all springing from the same ancestral pool of genetic variation.

Creationists deny that mutations fill the bill as the ultimate source of *new* variation. Mutations, they claim, are nearly always harmful and are, in any case, exceedingly rare—precisely the arguments seen as a serious intellectual challenge to Darwinian theory in genetics, until their resolution in the late 1920s and early 1930s. As we have already seen, genetic variation within species has recently been shown to exceed by far all previous estimates; and most mutations are small-scale and neither especially harmful nor beneficial when they occur. It fits the evolutionary view of the world that mutations are *random* with respect to the *needs* of organisms: mutations don't occur because they help an organism. They are, instead, mistakes in copying the genetic code—in this sense, no different from the mistakes monks occasionally made when copying medieval manuscripts. That some of these biological mistakes may ultimately prove beneficial is all evolutionists have ever claimed.

Kinds and Kinds: Creationists and the Hierarchy of Life

If evolution (according to creationists) goes on within but not between "kinds," their notion of "kind" becomes rather important. Creationists such as Parker and Gish openly admit that "kinds," or "basic kinds," are kind of hard to define. The word "kind" has no formal meaning in biology—though two hundred years ago Linnaeus used the Latin word for "kind"— "species"—for the lowest category in his hierarchical arrangement of life. Thus "kind" to a biologist, if it means anything at all, would mean species. Here is what Gish has to say about "basic kinds":

In the above discussion, we have defined a basic kind as including all of those variants which have been derived from a single stock. We have cited some examples of varieties which we believe should be included within a single basic kind. We cannot always be sure, however, what constitutes a separate kind. The division into kinds is easier the more the divergence observed. It is obvious, for example, that among invertebrates the protozoa, sponges, jellyfish, worms, snails, trilobites, lobsters, and bees are all different kinds. Among the vertebrates, the fishes, amphibians, reptiles, birds, and mammals are obviously different basic kinds.

Among the reptiles, the turtles, crocodiles, dinosaurs, pterosaurs (flying reptiles), and ichthyosaurs (aquatic reptiles) would be placed in different kinds. Each one of these major groups of reptiles could be further subdivided into the basic kinds within each.

Within the mammalian class, duck-billed platypuses, opossums, bats, hedgehogs, rats, rabbits, dogs, cats, lemurs, monkeys, apes, and men are easily assignable to different basic kinds. Among the apes, the gibbons, orangutans, chimpanzees, and gorillas would each be included in a different basic kind.

When we attempt to make fine divisions within groups of plants and animals where distinguishing features are subtle, there is a possibility of error. Many taxonomic distinctions established by man are uncertain and must remain tentative.

Let us now return to our discussion of evolution. According to the theory of evolution, not only have the minor variations within kinds arisen through natural processes, but the basic kinds themselves have arisen from fundamentally different ancestral forms. Creationists do not deny the former, that is, the origin of variations within kinds, but they do deny the latter, that is, the evolutionary origin of basically different types of plants and animals from common ancestors. (Gish, *Evolution: The Fossils Say No!*, pp. 34–35)

Gish, of course, cannot possibly mean what he literally says in this passage. He says that "variation" occurs within basic kinds but not between them—and proceeds to define such groups as "reptiles" and "mammals" as "basic kinds." By his very words, then, bats, whales, mankind, and the rest of the mammals he cites could have arisen as variations within the basic mammalian "kind." But he then defines these sub-groups of mammals as *themselves* constituting "basic kinds"—which means they cannot have shared a common ancestor by creationist tenets. Bats beget bats, whales beget whales, and so forth, but Gish implies there is no common ancestral connection between these basic sub-units of mammals. This, of course, is inconsistent at best and at worst senseless. One cannot but agree that creationists indeed have trouble with the notion of "basic kinds."

Gish points out that "division into kinds is easier the more the divergence observed"—whatever that might truly mean. What is obvious, instead, is that the closer we come to mankind, our own species *Homo sapiens,* the smaller the "basic kinds" Gish and other creationists wish to recognize. The invertebrate groups Gish lists are huge: "worms" include at least five phyla, snails constitute an entire class of mollusks (comparable at least to the vertebrate classes, such as birds and mammals), and trilobites are an arthropod class. Protozoa—one-celled, animal-like creatures—include many different phyla (according to some classifications).

The message is clear: let the paleontologist talk about evolution within the trilobite "kind." Trilobites arose early in the Cambrian Period, nearly six hundred million years ago, and are last found in rocks approximately 240 million years old. During their 350-million-year sojourn, we know of thousands of species that are classified into numerous families, superfamilies, and orders. But, apparently to creationists, if you've seen one trilobite you've seen them all, and all the changes paleontologists have documented in this important group of fossils are just "variation within a basic kind." I cannot agree. Trilobites are as diverse and prolific as the mammals, and examples of evolutionary change linking up two fundamental subdivisions of the "Class Trilobita" (I give one later in this chapter) are as compelling examples of evolution as any I know of. Airily dismissing 350 million years of trilobite evolution as "variation within a basic kind" is actually admitting that evolution, *substantial evolution,* has occurred.

But the real reason why creationists care little about trilobites is that they are really worried about only one "basic kind": mankind. I suspect that creationists would gladly define the rest of life as a single "basic kind" (and thus allow evolutionary connections between all forms of life) so long as mankind were singled out as a separate, unique "basic kind." After all, Arkansas Statute 590 makes a special point of defining a separate ancestry for man and apes as part of creation-science. And, as we shall see, a dominant concern underlying creationist efforts is the belief, sincerely held by some at least, that if we were to concede that man is an animal, descended from some more bestial form—an ape, a generalized primate, and so forth— there would be no reason for us to conduct ourselves in a moral way. Though Gish claims it is degree of "divergence" (which *sounds* evolutionary) that sets "basic kinds" apart, the degree of biochemical similarity between man and chimp was recently reported as greater than ninety-eight percent. It is a source of great satisfaction, I must admit, that with all the attention paid to the biology and fossil record of our own species (as Alexander Pope told us all along was only proper), it is far easier to demonstrate con-

nections between our own species—the "basic kind"
Homo sapiens—and other creatures, fossil and recent,
than it is to show connections between the major divisions of trilobites. More of that anon.

We are now in a position to compare the "scientific
creation model" of the origin of life's diversity with the
scientific notion of evolution. Creationists say there
can be variation within kinds ("microevolution") but
not between kinds ("macroevolution"—"real evolution" to Gary Parker). Biologists assert that there has
been one single history of life: all life has descended
from a single common ancestor; therefore one single
process—evolution—is responsible for the diversity we
see. Some evolutionists, myself among them, see it as
useful to make a distinction between microevolution
(small-scale, generation-by-generation change in gene
frequencies within populations) and macroevolution,
or the origin and diversification of groups classified
higher than species in the Linnaean hierarchy. But
here, as we have already seen, the debate within the
camp of real science centers on what ingredients (if
any) beyond pure natural selection working on variations within populations might be considered for a
complete theory of how the evolutionary process really
works. *All* evolutionary biologists share the common
goal of working toward a single, complete theory on
how life evolves. Creationists, in contrast, insist on two
separate theories: the creation of these nebulous "basic
kinds" by a supernatural Creator, followed by microevolution producing variation within those basic kinds.
They admit they have no scientific evidence for the
first phase. There is a commonly followed maxim that
the simpler idea in general is to be favored over a more
complex one when there is no compelling reason to
proceed otherwise. And the scientific-creation model
is a vastly more complex set of ideas than the simple
notion that all life descended from a single common
ancestor.

Oh, Those Gaps!

Creationists love "gaps"—lack of any obviously intermediate forms between dogs and cats, insectivores and bats, lizards and birds, fishes and frogs, and so on, and better yet their supposed absence in the fossil record. When naturalists, beginning with Aristotle, spoke of the "great chain of being," they drew attention to a continuity linking simple with complex, "lower" to "higher" forms of life, well before science had embraced the theory of evolution. And intermediate forms abound. There are arrays of similar species, closely related and barely distinguishable from one another—such as the South American fruit flies studied so intensively by Dobzhansky and his colleagues and students. (These don't count to creationists though, as it is merely "variation within kinds" to them.)

But there are intermediates on a grander scale as well. Most biologists would agree that our own mammalian Order, Primates, ranging from lemurs and lorises, South American monkeys, old world monkeys, the great apes, and man, is such a succession of intermediates. We share many basic features with apes; the apes and we together share further similarities with old world monkeys, and this group ("Anthropoidea") in turn shares further similarities with new world monkeys, and so forth. This is the familiar pattern discussed in Chapter 2—the predicted outcome of the evolutionary process. Old world monkeys are, in a very real sense, intermediate between more primitive Primates (prosimians and new world monkeys) and the Hominoidea: the great apes and man. What we see today are the survivors, with extinction knocking out other parts of the evolutionary chain that would (had they all survived) have formed an even tighter chain of interconnectedness within our order Primates.

But is is clear that one man's intermediate is another's "basic kind" or, failing that, outright fraud.

When it comes to the fossil record, we have already reviewed a bit of the checkered history that the vexatious problem of gaps has had in the annals of evolutionary biology. Paleontologists have, from time to time, blamed gaps solely or partly on the vagaries of the fossil record or have claimed that gaps, to the extent they are there at all, actually tell us something interesting about the nature of the evolutionary process. Few paleontologists (and none now active, as far as I am aware) have ever claimed that anatomically true intermediate forms actually never existed in the course of life's evolutionary history. Paleontologists, whatever their preferred explanation for why obviously intermediate forms are not found more frequently in the fossil record, always point to the intermediates that *have* been found as evidence that intermediates in fact existed. Creationists respond by refusing to accept the examples as intermediates. The stellar case is *Archaeopteryx,* the primitive animal so beautifully intermediate (to a scientist) between birds and advanced archosaurian reptiles. Creationists don't say *Archaeopteryx* is a fake: to them, it's just another bird. It isn't.

Archaeopteryx, currently known from five specimens, comes from Upper Jurassic limestones of Bavaria. The specimens are about 150 million years old. No earlier birds are known. Zoologists have known for years that birds are effectively feathered reptiles, as there are so relatively few anatomical differences between birds and living reptiles, and even fewer between birds and the archosaurian reptiles (including dinosaurs) of Mesozoic times. Birds lack teeth and have feathers, four-chambered hearts and horny bills, plus a few other characteristics not found in reptiles.

Gish says, "the so-called intermediate is no real intermediate at all because, as paleontologists acknowledge, *Archaeopteryx* was a true bird—it had wings, it was completely feathered, it *flew*. . . . It was not a half-way bird, it *was* a bird." (Gish, in *Evolution: The*

Fossils Say No!, p. 84; italics in original). In other words, since evolutionists classify *Archaeopteryx* as a bird, then a bird it is, not some kind of intermediate between birds and reptiles! Semantic games aside, it is certainly accurate to see birds as little more than feathered archosaurs. Feathers, wings, and a bill are three evolutionary novelties *Archaeopteryx* shares with all later birds, and these new features are the ones which allow us to recognize the evolutionary group "birds." But all living birds lack teeth and bony tails, and have well-developed keeled breastbones to support strong flight muscles. *Archaeopteryx* lacks such a keel, but still retains the teeth and bony tail typical of their reptilian ancestors.

The reason why *Archaeopteryx* delights paleontologists so is that evolutionary theory expects that new characteristics—the "evolutionary novelties" that define a group—will not appear all at the same time in the evolutionary history of the lineage. Some new characters will appear before others. Indeed, the entire concept of an intermediate hinges on this expectation. Creationists imply that any intermediate worthy of the name must exhibit an even gradation between primitive and advanced conditions of each and every anatomical feature. But there is no logical reason to demand of evolution that it smoothly modify all parts simultaneously. It is far more reasonable to expect that at each stage some features will be relatively more advanced than others; intermediates worthy of the name would have a mixture of primitive retentions of the ancestral condition, some in-between characters, and the fully evolved, advanced condition in yet other anatomical features. *Archaeopteryx* had feathered wings, but as yet the keeled sternum necessary for truly vigorous flight had not yet been developed in the avian lineage. And *Archaeopteryx* still had the reptilian tail, teeth, and claws on its wings.

Creationists point to some living birds that, while still young, have poorly developed keels or claws on their wings. They also point to Cretaceous birds, younger than *Archaeopteryx,* that still had teeth. Here is the height of twisted logic: creationists say, "Look here—here are modern and fossil birds out of the correct position in time, which also have some of the supposed intermediate or primitive reptilian features." Instead of interpreting these birds as primitive links to the past, creationists see them as somehow a challenge to *Archaeopteryx* as a gap-filling intermediate. The whole point about intermediates is that ancestral features are frequently retained while newer features are being added to another part of the body. It was not for another eighty million years or so that birds finally lost their teeth—though they *had* lost their tails in the meantime. And the fact that juvenile stages of descendants often show features of their adult ancestors—the observation that prompted Ernst Haeckel's famous nineteenth-century statement that "ontogeny recapitulates phylogeny" (meaning the evolutionary history of an animal is repeated in its development from egg to adult)—only serves to show the interrelatedness, the basic similarity, of all living things. Bluster as they might, creationists cannot wriggle out of *Archaeopteryx.*

But *Archaeopteryx* is simply the common showpiece example that intermediates between major groups of organisms do show up in the fossil record. All working systematists and paleontologists know of other, less celebrated, examples from their own work. Though I realize that creationists dub trilobites, the group with which I am most familiar, as a single "basic kind," thus at a stroke eliminating as irrelevant, examples of evolutionary change within trilobites, nonetheless I persist in thinking that patterns of change during the 350-million-year history of trilobites are germane to the question of gaps in the fossil record.

Trilobites, now extinct, were marine-dwelling arthropod relatives of crustaceans (such as crabs, lobsters, and shrimp) and chelicerates (such as horseshoe crabs

and spiders). Phacopid trilobites (Suborder Phacopina) first show up in rocks of Lower Ordovician age,
roughly 490 million years ago, and persisted until the
end of the Devonian Period, some 145 million years
later.

Phacopid trilobites are highly distinct. Their eyes are
typically faceted with large bulging lenses—lenses far
greater in size than those dotting the surface of insect,
crustacean, and other trilobite eyes. They have some
peculiar structures on the head ("facial sutures")
which look like those seen in the juveniles of other
trilobites. And the middle, flexible portion of their
bodies (the "thorax") always has eleven segments, no
more, no less. A highly distinctive group of trilobites,
paleontologists have wondered for over a hundred
years from what other group of trilobites the phacopids
sprung. What are their closest relatives? No one ever
found a suggestive intermediate.

In fact they had—though no one realized it for
over a century. It was not until more material of a
species first described in 1854 was collected, that
paleontologist Valdar Jaanusson realized the signif-
icance these fossils had for interpreting the origin of
the phacopids. In 1973, Jaanusson demonstrated that
this species, *Gyrometopus lineatus,* had the typical
number and anatomical configuration of true phacopid
thoracic segments, eyes intermediate between the phacopid "schizochroal" type and the "holochroal" form
found in virtually all other trilobites, and an additional
separate piece on the underside of the head—a piece
present in most trilobites, but unrecognizably fused
with other parts of the head in phacopids. Some, but
not all, of the advanced features which define the
Suborder Phacopina were present in this Lower Ordovician trilobite—and one of the advanced features
was actually in an intermediate condition.

The closest relatives of these phacopids have always
appeared to be cheirurids—trilobites with more thoracic segments than true phacopids (as a rule) and

primitive eyes—though cheirurids share with phacopids the "proparian" form of the facial suture. *Gyrometopus* retains a sort of cheirurid "leer," but even more convincing is the Ordovician cheirurid *Hammatocnemis,* described, during the past twenty years, from places as far-flung as Poland and China. The head of *Hammatocnemis* appears to be in the first stages of approaching the typical configuration found in true phacopids, and this trilobite affords yet another link in the chain between the more primitive cheirurids and the advanced phacopids—links that evolution-minded paleontologists knew must be there, but links that proved difficult to find because the specimens were so rare. *Hammatocnemis,* to be sure, is so far known only from Middle and Upper Ordovician rocks—too late to be *the* ancestors of *Gyrometopus* and other, more advanced, phacopids. But just as parents, as a rule, do not die when their children are born, so ancestors may live on alongside descendants: in fact, if ancestors did not live on in conservative lineages, we would not have amoebas, corals, and all the other myriad "lowly" forms of life still with us today. Intermediates are rare, but they do exist. Probably the best place to look for them these days is in museum drawers where more examples like Jaanusson's *Gyrometopus* are sure to be found.

I have saved the best till last. The creationists' main concern, the evolution of our own species, *Homo sapiens,* is their most difficult challenge. The most vexatious gaps in the fossil record are between groups ranked rather high in the Linnaean hierarchy. We, *Homo sapiens,* are but a single species, creationists' assertions about our constituting a "basic kind" notwithstanding. We are *much* more similar to apes than most other species are to their closest living relatives. And we have a pretty good fossil record which pushes our pedigree back a respectable four million years in time.

Paleontologists and anthropologists still debate—and

forever will continue to debate—the fine points of human evolution. Was it slow, steady, and gradual, or was it episodic? Were there more than one species at any one time, or was human evolution simply the progressive transformation of a single lineage through time? Nowhere else are passions more prominently displayed in the paleontological world—for the stakes are high. Nearly everyone, it seems, is interested in the latest finds from East Africa, and news of the latest Richard Leakey or Donald Johanson discovery is front-page news in *The New York Times*. Creationists are not alone in their preoccupation with the human side of the fossil record.

But with all the debates, all the angry turmoil, *all* combatants who are grinding their own axes over the human fossil record agree that, as you go back further and further into the rock record—as far back as four million years—fossils start out distinctly human, fully ourselves, and become smaller overall, smaller brained, and in general more apelike. *If* we shared a common ancestor with chimps and gorillas, *because* chimps and gorillas have smaller brains more nearly like other primate brains than ours, we predict that our mutual ancestor must have had a brain about chimp and gorilla size, and that there must have been an increase in brain size within our own lineage. The fossil record should show this increase in brain size. And it does.

Creationists fare poorly in the face of the tremendous amount of well-publicized information about the human fossil record. Their basic argument is weak. Creationists Gish and Parker agree with anthropologists that the more recent fossils are very modern in appearance, though they don't admit these humans appeared in Europe about thirty-five thousand years ago, and somewhat earlier in the Mideast and in Africa.

Then the creationists revive a discussion (still in vogue in some anthropological circles) that, with a necktie and coat on, a Neanderthal man would pass unnoticed in the New York subways. Perhaps—I doubt it, but Neanderthals *are* considered simply a subspecies of our own *Homo sapiens.* Creationists, of course, do not accept the dates of 100,000–35,000 years for the time Neanderthals were walking around.

Skipping back 1.5 million years or so, we find the Australopithecines, whose name means (as creationists fondly point out) "southern apes"—and automatically in the creationist book, a form of ape, and no member of the human lineage. Assessing zoological relationships on such etymological grounds is rather dubious, to say the least—but the creationists' "it looks like an ape so call it an ape" judgment greatly insults these remote ancestors and collateral kin of ours. Their brains were advanced both in size and complexity relative to apes' brains. They had upright posture, a bipedal gait, and some of them, at least, fashioned tools in a distinctive style. No apes these—but primitive hominids looking and acting just about the way you would expect them to so soon after our lineage split off from the line that became the modern great apes.

But it is the fossils of the middle 1.5 million years that I just skipped over that make creationists writhe. Here we have *Homo erectus,* first known to the world as *Pithecanthropus erectus* ("erect ape man"—based on specimens from Java) and as *Sinanthropus pekinensis* ("Peking man"). Now known from Africa as well, *Homo erectus* lived on virtually unchanged for over 1.5 million years (according to some anthropologists) and was, by all appearances, a singularly successful species. They had fire and made elaborate stone tools. And they had a brain size intermediate between the older African fossils and the later, modern-looking, specimens. Specimens of *Homo erectus* don't look like apes, yet they don't look exactly like us, either. To most of us, *Homo erectus* looks exactly like an intermediate between ourselves and our more remote ancestors.

What do creationists do with *Homo erectus?* No problem—*Homo erectus* is a fake in the creationist lexicon. Gish asks us to recall Piltdown, that famous forgery—evidence of skullduggery in the ranks of learned academe. And what, they ask, about *Hesperopithecus haroldcookii*—"Nebraska man," described years ago on the basis of a single tooth which later turned out to have belonged to a pig! (Scientists *do* make mistakes—and pig and human molars are rather similar, presumably a reflection of similar diets.) So it is, they say, with *Homo erectus*. According to Gish, the Java fossils were just skull caps of apes wrongly associated with a modern human thigh bone. And the original Peking fossils were studied primarily by one man (Franz Weidenreich) who, Gish suspects, "was guilty of the same lack of objectivity and preconceived ideas that motivated Black." (*Evolution: The Fossils Say No!*, p. 126). Evidently, as an evolutionist, Weidenreich was not to be trusted. *And,* what's more, the fossils are now gone—supposedly lost by a contingent of U.S. marines evacuating China in the face of the Japanese invasion of World War II. Hmmm, very suspicious, all this. Never mind the casts of the originals, the drawings and photographs of these fossils in Weidenreich's memoirs. Never mind that the Chinese have since found more skulls at the original site, or that Richard Leakey has found the same species, beautifully preserved, in East Africa.

That the best the creationists can do with the human fossil record is call the most recent fossils fully human, the earliest merely apes, and those in the middle—the intermediates, if you will—outright fakes is pathetic. Humans are about the worst example of a "basic kind" creationists could have chosen. Creationists would do far better with trilobites. But they don't especially care about trilobites. They care about human evolution, and the fossil record there is a steady stream of intermediates. The irony is great: the case toward which all their passion for producing propaganda is ultimately directed—how *we* got here—is about the most difficult one I can think of to support the "model" of Creation.

More on the Creationists on the Fossil Record

Creationists, like other human beings, like to have their cake and eat it too. Their use of the fossil record is a stunning example of having it both ways: the sequence of fossils, the manner of their appearance in the strata, and the gaps between "basic kinds" all refute evolution, they say. But, as we have already seen, creationists also say that there is really no sequence at all—the entire stratigraphic record, with all its fossils, was formed in one cataclysmic, epochal Flood, which lasted a mere forty days.

Gish cites the Cambrian explosion of life (which we reviewed in detail in Chapter 3 as an example of the general nature, complexities, and problems of the fossil record) as a prime example of Creation. Gish says that the sudden appearance of all those complex, diversified animals falsifies evolution and is just what one would expect from the "Creation model." Yet the "Creation model" entails a brief (six twenty-four-hour days—not in the Arkansas Statute, but in all the prominent creationist tracts) period of Creation. One would certainly expect there to be no sequence of life in the rock layers: *all* forms of life, as we know them today, should appear at the base of the Cambrian. Creationist paleontologists, such as Georges Cuvier in the first half of the nineteenth century, had to invoke multiple creations to make the rock record fit creationist beliefs. The extreme creationists today are unwilling to bend that far: all change after the Cambrian was "within basic kinds"—but also, at one and the same time, there was no Cambrian and there was no change because the entire fossil record was formed by (1) ecological zonation, (2) hydraulic sorting, and (3) relative capacity of different organisms to flee advancing flood waters. Creationists have two entirely different and utterly conflicting explanations of the fossil record—and both can be found within the confines of single books such as Parker's *Creation: The Facts of Life* and Gish's *Evolution: The Fossils Say No!* Somehow, as difficult as the Cambrian explosion is to understand in scientific terms, the explanations of geologists and paleontologists seem to me far more compelling than the meager creationist efforts. The Cambrian "explosion" actually involved fifteen million years of time. And the closest relatives of each of the hard-shelled invertebrates that enter the fossil record back then are soft-bodied in every case: arthropods, with trilobites as their most primitive members, are most closely related to soft-bodied, segmented worms. Corals are most closely allied to sea anemones. And so on. We don't see much evidence of intermediates in the Early Cambrian because the intermediates had to have been soft-bodied, and thus extremely unlikely to become fossilized. And to admit puzzlement over some aspects of life's history, as paleontologists still partly, and frankly, do in the case of the Lower Cambrian, is a far more prudent course than the double-headed, inconsistent gobbledygook propounded by creationists as a rational, "scientific" alternative.

Earlier I said that creationists are poor scholars at best and at worst have been known to distort the words and works of scientists. Anthropologist Laurie Godfrey (writing in the June 1980 issue of *Natural History*) has documented many examples of creationists' penchant to twist words and evidence to suit their purpose. I cannot close this discussion of creationist views of the fossil record without documenting this serious charge a bit further.

The ICR's Gary Parker has been among the more blatant offenders. On page 95 of his *Creation: The Facts of Life,* we read: "Famous paleontologists at Harvard, the American Museum, and even the British Museum say we have *not a single* example of evolutionary transition at all." This is untrue. A prominent creationist interviewed a number of paleontologists at those institutions and elsewhere (actually, he never did get to Harvard). I was one of them. Some of us candidly admitted that there are some procedural difficulties in recognizing ancestors and that, yes, the fossil record is rather full of gaps. Nothing new there. This creationist then wrote letters to various newspapers, and even testified at hearings that the paleontologists he interviewed admitted that there are no intermediates in the fossil record. Thus, the lie has been perpetuated by Parker. All of the paleontologists interviewed have told me that they did cite examples of intermediates to the interviewer. The statement is an outright distortion of the willing admission by paleontologists concerned with accuracy that, to be sure, there are gaps in the fossil record. Such is creationist "scholarship."

One final word about creationists and fossils: it would certainly be helpful to the creationist cause if all organisms could be shown to have appeared at the same time in the rock record. Thus their delight at the supposed human footprints alongside *bona fide* dinosaur tracks in the Cretaceous Glen Rose Formation, exposed in the channel of the Paluxy River in Texas. Here, they proclaim, is direct evidence that man and dinosaur roamed the earth together, just as it was written in Alley Oop. Parker is quite suave as he describes fitting his own feet into these impressions. But none other than a creationist (B. Neufeld, *Dinosaur Tracks and Giant Men,* 1975) has blown the whistle on these tracks. Alas for the creationist cause, they aren't footprints at all; the few impressions visible these days do not show any signs of "squishing" of the sedimentary layers either at the edges or directly beneath the "tracks" (as the dinosaur prints, incidentally, clearly do). And, according to Neufeld, during the Depression years it was a common local practice to chisel out human footprints to enhance tourist interest—a practice akin to the recent fabrication of "Sasquatch" footprints in the Pacific Northwest. Need anything more be said about the quality and trustworthiness of creationists' dealings with the fossil record?

Design, Chance, and Complexity

Creationist authors have devoted whole books to their interpretations of the data of biology. But apart from their convoluted arguments about fossils and "basic kinds," it turns out they find relatively little in biology that they can offer as supportive of the "Creation model." What little there is of substance (if it can be called such) centers around the notions of design, chance, and complexity.

One of Darwin's first and most persistent critics after *The Origin* appeared was St. George Mivart. Mivart hounded Darwin on a problem he was already amply troubled with: How could one imagine a structure as complex and beautifully suited to perform its function as a human eye to have evolved through a series of simpler, less useful and efficient stages? Anatomists were among the last holdouts against accepting the idea of evolution, so entranced were they with the intricate complexities of the organ systems they studied. Imagining intermediate stages between, say, the front leg of a running reptile and the perfected wing of a bird seemed to them impossible, as it still does to today's creationists. That the problem perhaps reflects more the poverty of human imagination than any real constraint on nature is an answer not congenial to the creationist line of thought.

Interwoven with the difficulty in imagining the gradual evolution of complex organs are two separate themes: the more complex a structure is, the more eloquent a silent argument it is for the conscious work of a Designer. And the more complex a structure, the more improbable that it arose by "chance alone." Creationists go to town with both themes.

The argument that nature is so complexly organized,

with each creature specially suited to the role it plays in the economy of nature that only a Creator could have fashioned things this way, is an old one, ante-dating Garner Ted Armstrong's use of the grunions by at least two centuries. It was the particular view of the theologian–naturalists prior to *The Origin,* and it is still in use today in the creationist literature. Creationists usually talk of watches (though Gary Parker prefers Boeing 747s). Such complex machines, so admirably suited to the purpose they serve, require a watchmaker. All the parts must be premeditatedly put together by an expert craftsman. Alone, no spring or jewel can keep the time. Only when the watchmaker cleverly ar-ranges the parts in precisely the right way does the watch become functional. Clearly, the very existence of watches directly implies the existence of a watch-maker.

So, too, creationists argue, does the existence of complex organisms imply a conscious Creator. Hearts and hands alone do not a person make—they must be organized, assembled in just the right way to produce a functional human being—though, of course, it is the perfectly naturalistic translation of the genetic code that fashions and assembles the parts of organisms. Parker says of such arguments from design that "You don't have to see the Creator, and you don't have to see the creative act to recognize evidence of creation." (in *Creation: The Facts of Life,* p. 4.) Later Parker writes: "Creation is based instead (i.e., instead of imagination) on *logical inference* from our *scientific observations,* and on simple acknowledgment that everyone, scientists and laymen alike, recognize that certain kinds of order imply a Creator" (p. 16; italics in original).

Now, as a scientist, I'll grant that a Boeing 747 im-plies a creator. I've seen pictures of the assembly line and, more to the point, as a scientist I am aware that the aluminum it is made from is extracted (with great difficulty and expenditure of energy) from its

complex ore—a process known only, insofar as I am
aware, to human beings. And so on. I will further
admit that, lacking a cogent alternative like evolution,
the analogy with organisms (that they, too, bespeak a
knowledgeable, conscious intelligence behind them)
was a plausible argument—for the 1820s. But how
compelling is the analogy today? The argument boils
down simply to this: we can invoke a naturalistic
process, evolution, for which there is a great deal of
evidence, but which we still have some difficulties in
fully comprehending. Or we can say, simply, that some
Creator did it and we are, after all, only watches (perhaps an insight, after all, into what makes creationists
tick). The analogy is as meaningless as that: it
"proves" nothing. It could even be true—but it cannot
be construed as science, it isn't biology, and in the
end it amounts to nothing more than a simple assertion
that naturalistic processes automatically *cannot* be considered as candidates for an explanation of the order
and complexity we all agree we do see in nature.

To bolster the argument from design, creationists
jump to the other side of the complexity argument:
evolution just could not, they say, produce these organic complexities because there is no way such complex structural systems could have developed by
"chance alone." Just as a bunch of monkeys endlessly
pounding typewriters would never duplicate the works
of Shakespeare, no mindless, materialistic process such
as evolution—portrayed as acting by blind chance
alone—could ever have produced the myriad wonders
of the organic realm.

But evolutionary theorists are not the simpletons
such statements would make them out to be. As we
have seen, the dominant form of evolutionary theory
these past fifty years, the "modern synthesis," has been
almost rigidly dogmatic on just this very point: mutations are random, but random only with respect to the
needs of an organism. But mutations are caused by real
physico-chemical processes, and there is a limited num-

ber of forms that a mutation can take and still function
as a viable gene. And then there is natural selection—
typically portrayed (by biologists) as the vigilant monitor of environmental change, constantly picking only
the most beneficial of the variations present in a generation to ensure their transmittal to the next generation.
This view of natural selection is statistical—but nonetheless highly deterministic. It is, in fact, the evolutionary naturalistic alternative to a Creator. And
though recently some biologists have seen a larger role
for random factors in evolution, and the central, om-
nipotent role of natural selection has been questioned
by others, natural selection has the advantage over a
Creator (i.e., *as a purely scientific question*) because it
has a good deal of empirical evidence going for it.
Chance, design, and complexity are handled well, if not
always stunningly, by evolutionary theory and in biological observation and experimentation—sufficiently
well, on the one hand, to be scientific and *not* to require the *ad hoc* intervention of a supernatural Creator,
on the other.

The Creationists' Last Card: The Origin of Life

What about the origin of life? For creationists, the
origin of complex, self-replicating living systems from
the inorganic realm demands the action of improbable
chance, and implies a Creator. Pointing to the in-
ability of biochemists to synthesize life in a test tube,
creationists agree with the poet: only God can make
a tree. Only a Creator could have assembled all those
complex ingredients of DNA, house them in a pro-
teinaceous sheath, and thus fashion the first primitive
form of life.

Evolutionists commonly respond that complex "organic" molecules occur throughout the universe and
many (such as amino acids, the building blocks of

proteins) can be synthesized simply by passing a spark through a gaseous mixture of ammonia, methane, hydrogen, and water—as was first done by Stanley Miller in the 1950s using the ingredients thought to be the main atmospheric constituents of the primitive earth. Creationists counter that such results are far removed from producing true life. Biologists, of course, agree, while maintaining that such experiments are both supportive and suggestive of the hypothesis that life did, indeed, arise from natural processes.

Some biologists, such as Nobel Laureate Francis Crick, do stress the great difficulties involved in the origin of, say, the molecules of inheritance and protein synthesis—DNA and RNA—from simpler, and ultimately inorganic, systems. Such biologists seriously doubt the ubiquity of life throughout the universe as envisioned by some cosmologists, who argue that an improbable event becomes probable given enough tries: there are billions of stars in the universe, and so, one may suppose, many planets with conditions similar to our own on which life may well have developed independently. Neither argument is particularly compelling in the absence of any hard information. But it is important to note in passing that whether or not life arose on earth, or arose elsewhere and spread here (a view favored by Crick, for example), both sides agree that once bacteria became established on earth, all of the rest of life, as we know it, evolved from them.

It is true that DNA is complex. It is true that no one has taken primordial compounds supposedly in the earth's primitive atmosphere and created DNA—much less a functional bacterium—in the laboratory. The creationists wish us to suppose this situation demonstrates that life *cannot* have arisen by natural processes. I can't follow their argument: in the brief history of biochemistry we have gone from laborious analysis of what proteins are, through the cracking of the genetic code (by Crick among others), to the heady days of gene-splicing and cloning. That the origin of life, if posed as a biochemical problem, remains incompletely solved as of 1981 is not particularly surprising and certainly not compelling evidence that it never will be. But if we are to continue to teach our children that such problems are beyond the purview of science because "the Creator did it," we certainly will lessen our chances of ever finding out.

What You See Is What You Get: The Creator Did It

There must be a single, hierarchically arranged pattern of resemblance interlinking all life *if* all life descended from a single common ancestor. This is evolution's grand prediction. As we have seen, the prediction has been constantly tested for over a century and abundantly corroborated. Moreover, this prediction provides the basic rationale for biomedical and agricultural research. What do the creationists have to say in answer?

Most creationists simply affirm that it pleased the Creator to fashion life in the form in which we find it today. As to why some organisms share more similarities with each other than they do to others, creationists give two answers: variation within "basic kinds" by microevolution explains some of the similarity, while the notion that the Creator was efficient and used the same blueprint for the separately created "basic kinds" explains why mammals, birds, reptiles, and amphibians all have one upper and two lower leg bones (except, of course, in snakes and other secondarily limbless "tetrapods").

At least one creationist has gone beyond these usual arguments: Gary Parker (in *Creation: The Facts of Life*) has denied that there really is a single, nested pattern of similarity interconnecting all life. Parker writes (alluding to patterns of similarity in different

organ systems in lizards, but clearly generalizing), "The
pattern is not a branching one suggesting evolutionary
descent from a common ancestor; rather, it is a mosaic
pattern . . . suggesting creation according to a common
plan" (p. 22).

I am relieved. Parker's "mosaic pattern" allows absolutely no predictions about the distribution of similarities in the organic realm. Bats may share similar
dental patterns with shrews, but if we look at their
blood, who knows? Perhaps bats will prove to be
more similar to beetles. "As far as creationists are
concerned, hemoglobin occurs, complete and fully
functional, wherever it is appropriate in the Creator's
total plan, somewhat like a blue-colored tile in an
artist's mosaic" (*op. cit.,* p. 20). Forget the monkeys
and apes for testing drugs ultimately intended for
humans. Perhaps our inner biochemical workings are
more similar to those of crayfish. We need look no further into creationist notions of biology for signs of true
science: if you cannot make predictions about what
you might expect to find when you look at an organism, you cannot be doing science with that organism.

So, in the end, there is as little of substance in the
scientific creationist treatment of the origin and diversification of life as there is in their treatment of cos-
mological time. They pose no testable hypotheses and
make no predictions or observations worthy of the
name. They devote the vast bulk of their ponderous
efforts to attacking orthodox science in the mistaken
and utterly fallacious belief that in discrediting science
(or, as they put it, "evolution-science") they have
thereby established the truth of their own position.
Their efforts along these particular lines are puny.
Moreover, they impugn the integrity and intelligence of
thousands of honest souls who have had the temerity to
believe that it is both fitting and proper to try to
understand the universe, the earth and all its life in
naturalistic terms, using only the evidence of our senses
to evaluate how truthful an idea might be. Yes, his-

torical geology and evolutionary biology are sciences. They are imperfect—but self-correcting. And, no, scientific creationism is not science—not by any conceivable stretching of the term. It remains to be seen exactly what creationism, including "special creationism" and "scientific creationism," *really* is: nothing but that good, old-time religion.

Chapter 7

CREATIONISM, RELIGION, AND POLITICS

CREATIONISTS THESE DAYS ARE VERY CAREFUL NOT TO bring God, Christ, or any religious tenet directly into their characterization of the creation model. But they are fooling no one when they proffer their scientific creationism, and even casual perusal of recent numbers of *Acts and Facts* (the ICR's newsletter) reveals a dedicated commitment to a fundamentalist Protestant brand of Christianity. So-called public school editions of recent creationist books, in which the authors have striven mightily to expunge all religious references to satisfy the U.S. Constitution, are nonetheless peppered with religious allusions. The overtly religious editions intended for sectarian private schools are simply the same books that have "come out of the closet."

The definition of creation-science in Arkansas Statute 590, as we have seen, is very similar to lawyer Wendell Bird's characterization of the scientific-creation model in the December 1978 issue of *Acts and Facts*. But Bird's original purpose in that article was to contrast *two* creation models: the "scientific creation" version and the "Biblical creation model." The similarities between the two are compelling. Instead of "Special creation of the universe and earth (by a

Creator) on the basis of scientific evidence," point one
of his "Biblical creation model" reads: "Divine creation of the heaven, stars, and earth by God, on the
basis of Genesis." And so on down his list of seven
points (reduced to six in the statute). Instead of entropy (i.e., invocation of the Second Law of Thermodynamics to produce deterioration), point two of the
"Biblical creation model" speaks of "application of
the curse, pronounced by God after Adam's fall, to
produce deterioration in the earth and life." All points
repeat "on the basis of Genesis," rather than "on the
basis of scientific evidence."

Similarly, Henry Morris (*Acts and Facts,* July 1980)
writes that "Creationism can be studied and taught in
any of three basic forms, as follows: (1) Scientific
creationism (no reliance on Biblical revelation, utilizing
only scientific data to support and expound the creation
model). (2) Biblical creationism (no reliance on scientific data, using *only the Bible* to expound and defend
the creation model). (3) Scientific Biblical creationism
(full reliance on *Biblical revelation* but *also* using
scientific data to support and develop the creation
model)" (italics in original). *The* creation model!
Morris is clearly saying that the creationist position
can be interchangeably considered religion, science, or
a mixture of the two—depending upon the intended
audience. Substituting "the curse" for "entropy" is
merely semantic chicanery, not a serious intellectual
enterprise. The nineteenth-century scientists who were
true creationists took both their faith and their interpretation of nature from the Bible, and there never has
been any other source of inspiration or support for the
"creation model."

Religious leaders are understandably alarmed at recent creationist advances. Freedom to practice religion—any religion—is one of the dearest rights Americans have. Such pluralistic tolerance can only be had
in a secular society, where the state has no vested interest in any single religious view. No one is more

aware of the importance of the separation of church and state than the clergy, and it is no coincidence that many of the plaintiffs in the recent court challenge to the Arkansas statute were prominent members of the Arkansas religious community.

But the creationist effort is religiously troubling on another level as well. As I recently heard a young minister from Georgia put it, creationists trivialize religion, demeaning it by insisting it be viewed as a strict alternative to science. Religion has a multiplicity of functions in society, and for *some* religious people, an explanation of how things have come to be as they are may be one of them. But the main function of all religions centers on the spiritual well-being of their followers—their hopes and ethics, their world view: What do we make of life? How can we understand its meaning and purpose? Most of us don't pin our personal resolution of the thorny problems of life's meaning on which view we adopt about how the earth got here. Few of us see the ethical fabric of human social behavior as dependent upon one scenario or another about how we humans got here in the first place. But creationists *do* look upon things this way—and therein lies, I think, the source of all that zeal in the creationist movement.

Judge Braswell Deen, of the Georgia Court of Appeals, in a quote that has become rather famous, recently charged that "this monkey mythology of Darwin is the cause of permissiveness, promiscuity, pills, prophylactics, perversions, pregnancies, abortions, pornotherapy, pollution, poisoning, and proliferation of crimes of all types." And during the "Scopes II" trial, Nell Segraves (the plaintiff's mother and a director of the Creation Research Center in San Diego) had the following exchange with Robert Bazell, science reporter for "NBC Nightly News": Bazell: "For seventeen years since the Supreme Court banned prayer in public schools, Mrs. Segraves has been fighting to bring religion back to the schools. She believes that the teaching of evolution is the primary evil, responsible for all sorts of problems." Segraves: "What about prostitution, or the drugs, or the criminal activities, violence. It's lack of respect." Bazell: "And you think that all that can be traced to the teaching of evolution in the schools?" Segraves: "I believe it can, and I think I can prove it." Now it is surely an irony that the Old Testament amply documents the presence of many of the same social ills (and plenty more) plaguing Jewish society thousands of years ago, yet nothing is said of their teaching evolution to their children.

But creationists are sincere in their belief that evolution is one of Satan's more potent weapons against the forces of good. Creationist R. L. Wysong is quite explicit on the reason why. In his *The Creation–Evolution Controversy*—in which Wysong affects an unbiased stance (unsuccessfully, in my opinion)—he explains the importance of the controversy: one's position on "origins" frames one's world view, and one's world view, in turn, leads to one's "approach to life." A "correct" position on origins leads to a "correct" world view which, in turn, leads to solutions to life's problems. "A person can basically take one of two positions on origins. One is there is a creator, the other is there is not; or, evolution explains origins or it does not. Creation versus evolution, theism versus materialism or naturalism, and design versus chance, are all ways of expressing the two alternatives. (I will demonstrate the fallacy of so-called theistic evolution, which is held by some as a third alternative, in a later chapter)" (Wysong, pp. 5–6). Wysong goes on to argue that the evolutionary position influenced the thinking of such historical figures as Marx, Mussolini, Hitler, and Freud. But "if, on the other hand, life owes its existence to a creator, a supernatural force, then life is the result of his will and purposes. Understanding these purposes would be the only way to understand life's varied questions and problems" (Wysong, p. 9).

A woman in Philadelphia, in a letter to me, put it

even more bluntly: Greatly mistaking my position (taken from a newspaper article), she wrote to thank me for my efforts in combating the notion that we humans have descended from lower forms of life, for were we to teach that to our children, we could not expect them to conduct themselves in a moral way. One need not be a "materialist" to note that a functioning society demands such behavior—and that there are other, more compelling, explanations for why we are, collectively, less than perfect in our ability always to behave in the very best way. But such is the creationist belief, and the reason for their persistence is, far more than the urge for fame or the slight profit motive attributable at least to some creationists, their conviction that evolution undermines morality. That Wysong's "third alternative"—theistic evolution, or the belief in a Creator-God who fashioned the universe, earth, and life using His natural laws—is anathema to these purists can only mean one thing: despite their protestations that they are only looking at the scientific evidence, creationists at heart are fundamentalists who must insist on the inerrancy of the Bible. And "theistic evolution," which allows a metaphorical interpretation of biblical stories, simply collides with the literal interpretation demanded by fundamentalism.

So creationism is simply one of the more visible fronts of the war against "secular humanism." Indeed, it is the ethical (materialistic) implications of evolution that drive most creationists wild, and I have already remarked that such a naturalistic explanation of life's diversity troubled Darwin too, as well as many an evolutionist after him. And it is true that some thinkers through the years have endeavored to draw moral and ethical implications from the notion of evolution. Most of such thought has come from mystics and philosophers. Some of it has come from evolutionary biologists. But if evolution has served as the basis of the peculiar ethics of some individuals, does that make evolution a "religion," as some creationists claim? Certainly not—though this is precisely what Nell Segraves & Co. argued in their "Scopes II" case in California early in 1981. To the Segraves, creationism isn't science so much as evolution is religion—an aspect, if you will, of the more general religion of "secular humanism." But no practicing scientists invoke the supernatural in their work—a cardinal rule of the trade—whereas all religions worthy of the name *do* embrace a concept of the supernatural. Nor, to my knowledge, are any of the trappings, be they ideological or materialistic, of organized religion to be found in the realm of evolutionary biology. That biologists these days continue to see no alternative to evolution as an explanation of how we got here is far from sufficient grounds for labeling the practice of evolutionary biology a "religion."

The Battle in the Body Politic

The Supreme Court, after a good long time, has finally held that all the old "monkey laws" which forbade the teaching of evolution are unconstitutional. The task in the current litigation against the newly enacted "equal time" bills in Arkansas and Louisiana is to show that creation-science is a wolf in sheep's clothing, and is really a highly sectarian religious belief masquerading as science. Since this is patently the case, it seems unlikely that state (or national) legislation will ultimately prove successful in the creationist effort.

Creationists nowadays claim the equal-time laws broaden the range of material presented to students and that a student's right to know, is, in effect, abridged if he is denied instruction in the "creation model." I have said enough, I think, to show that the creation model is essentially religion, and thus inappropriate in a biology classroom; and, to the extent that the creation model contains any science, it is outmoded,

already falsified science. And we simply cannot teach
each outmoded idea in science as if it were still to be
considered a valid alternative explanation.

On the other hand, creationists argue that it is an
infringement of a student's rights to practice religion
freely if a student is taught only evolution in the classroom. But no science instructor should ever teach anything as if it were the final truth. And students should
learn only what scientists think evolution is and how
it works—and why these things are so. Students should
not be asked to "believe," but they *should* be taught
those things, such as evolution, that scientists think are
true of the natural universe.

The actions of legislatures and courts of law attract
a great deal of attention, and are important at least as
much in shaping public opinion as for their actions
per se. The Segraves family lost "Scopes II" in a
technical sense but gained much in notoriety and thus
attracted additional grass-roots support for their cause.
If I am optimistic about the outcome of future court
cases, I am nonetheless sickened by the evidence of
real creationist successes in the minds of the American
public, who in turn pressure local school boards, offi-
cials, and teachers.

Here are the results of a recent reader survey con-
ducted by *Glamour* magazine: "Do you believe in Darwin's theory of evolution?" No—fifty-three percent;
Yes—forty-seven percent. "If Darwin's theory of evolution is taught in public schools, should other views
(including the divine origin of life) be taught too?"
Yes—seventy-four percent; No—twenty-six percent.
"Do you think that scientists are right in their argument that by giving creationism equal time they are
allowing religion into the public schools?" No—fifty-
six percent; Yes—forty-four percent. "If you think
Darwinism and creationism are both valid theories,
what is the best way to teach them?" "Sixty-one percent say change the textbooks or school curricula,
seventeen percent say teach creationism at home, nine

percent say all students should be required to take courses in biology and religion, and thirteen percent say 'other.' "

Now it may be supposed that the respondents were mainly people with strong opinions on the subject—and there are far more people passionately committed to creationism than there are devotees of evolution (or nuclear physics or any other branch of science). Nonetheless, the results of this poll are disconcerting. Creationists have been making truly great inroads. How can they be thwarted?

All of us concerned with the quality of American education had better focus on the activities in our local school districts. Sometimes school boards are petitioned for curriculum changes, while sometimes it is individual teachers who unilaterally introduce creationism (or quietly drop evolution) in their courses of study. Most science teachers, though, are dead set against teaching creationism, but need support from the community at large. Fight fire with fire—for every apologist trying to inject religion into the science curriculum in the name of scientific creationism, there should be two or more of us ready to get up and call it what it is—sectarian religious belief. Some school boards around the country have recently turned to a rather expedient, and I think fair, way of dealing with the creationist onslaught: creationism is handled (either in an entirely separate course or as a segment of the social studies curriculum) as part of a discussion of different notions of origins—in which case the tenets of many of the world's religions are brought in, as well as the Judaeo-Christian story. And in any case, it would always be proper for a science teacher to acknowledge that creationism exists at the outset of the evolution part of a biology course, but then to drop creationism (because it is religion) and teach evolution as an idea—albeit an extraordinarily powerful, and the only idea currently held by science on the matter of biological "origins."

The growing alarm generated by the sweeping attack on "secular humanism" has sparked the formation of a number of organizations dedicated to resisting the infringements of liberties sought by this militant neopopulist "new right." Specifically focusing on creationism, "committees of correspondence" (the name comes from Thomas Paine's confederation of organizations in the Thirteen Colonies) have been formed in over thirty-five states. These committees, whose members include scientists, clergymen, teachers, and parents, monitor statewide legislative action, organize workshops and symposia on creationism, and aid anticreationists in local battles in the public schools. Similarly, teachers' organizations have become alarmed and are also making concerted efforts to fight this spread of pseudoscience.

In the end, the evolution/creationism controversy is a battle over public opinion. It hasn't been an intellectual problem for a least a century. And today we have legislatures determining what is and is not science, and what the content of science really is—in a manner about as remote from any recognizable intellectual activity as one could imagine. So it is strictly in the area of public opinion that the battle is really being fought. Anticreationists do not need to tout a "belief" in evolution, nor should we seek to inculcate our children with such a belief. But we must insist on the integrity of our children's education in science: for scientific illiteracy will send the United States on a surer and straighter path to hell than ever will that idea we call evolution.

BIBLIOGRAPHY

BIBLIOGRAPHY

Works Discussed in This Book

Darwin, Charles. 1859. *On the Origin of Species*. John Murray, London. The classic. The sixth edition is the most commonly available nowadays. A facsimile of the first edition is available from Atheneum.

Dobzhansky, Theodosius. 1937. *Genetics and the Origin of Species*. Columbia University Press. Later editions (1941, 1951) trace the development of Dobzhansky's thought. The original edition is perhaps the central document of the "synthetic theory" of evolution. It has been recently (1982) reprinted by Columbia.

Freske, Stanley. 1981. "Creationist Misunderstanding, Misrepresentation, and Misuse of the Second Law of Thermodynamics." *Creation/Evolution,* Issue IV. A penetrating essay from the only journal devoted to the current controversy between science and creationism.

Gish, Duane T. 1978. *Evolution: The Fossils Say No!* Public School Edition. Creation-Life Publishers. Enough said.

Godfrey, Laurie. 1981. "The Flood of Evolutionism." *Natural History,* Vol. 90, No. 6. A highly readable essay on a serious subject: creationist distortions of scientific writings.

Mayr, Ernst. 1942. *Systematics and the Origin of Species*. Columbia University Press (reprinted, 1982). Another important book on the evolutionary synthesis, by one of its founders.

Morris, Henry M. 1963. *The Twilight of Evolution*. Presbyterian and Reformed Publishing Company. Contains some of the more quotable creationist material—written before it became unfashionable for creationists openly to admit their religious motivations.

————. 1977. *The Scientific Case for Creation*. Creation-Life Publishers. A typical effort by creationism's chief proponent.

Neufeld, B. 1975. "Dinosaur Tracks and Giant Men." *Origins,* Vol. 2. A creationist takes a skeptical look at the Glen Rose footprints.

Parker, Gary. 1980. *Creation: The Facts of Life*. Creation-Life Publishers. A creationist looks at biology.

Read, John G. (with assistance from C. L. Burdick). 1979. *Fossils, Strata and Evolution*. Scientific-Technical Presentations. Creationists look at thrust faults, the geologic column, and evolution.

Ross, C. P., and Richard Rezak. 1959. *The Rocks and Fossils of Glacier National Monument*. U.S. Geological Survey Professional Paper 294-K. A technical account of, among other things, the famous "Lewis overthrust," where Precambrian-aged rocks sit atop Cretaceous sediments in the northwestern United States.

Simpson, George Gaylord. 1944. *Tempo and Mode in Evolution*. Columbia University Press. The book that integrated the data of the fossil record with genetics in the 1940s.

Weber, Christopher G. 1980. "Common Creationist Attacks on Geology." *Creation/Evolution*, Issue II. A handy summary of what some creationists say, and what to reply to them, on matters geological.

Whitcomb, John C., and Henry M. Morris. 1961. *Genesis Flood*. Presbyterian and Reformed Publishing Company. The name says it all.

Wysong, R. L. 1976. *The Creation–Evolution Controversy*. Inquiry Press. Not the impartial examination of both sides it claims to be, nonetheless this is perhaps the most thorough and densely argued of all creationist efforts to date.

Suggestions for Further Reading

The creationists have been very successful in promoting their literature, so I will not aid them further by listing material in addition to the sources I have quoted in this book. I have cited two issues of *Acts and Facts,* a newsletter published regularly by the Institute for Creation Research (a division of Christian Heritage College), San Diego, California.

The scientific community has been slow to react to the current creationist onslaught, and little of the literature listed below has been written with creationism firmly in mind. A number of books on creationism by scientists and educators are currently in the works. The references listed here should provide a good source for anyone wishing to pursue modern thinking in anthropology, astronomy, biology, and geology.

Cloud, Preston. 1978. *Cosmos, Earth and Man: A Short History of the Universe*. Yale University Press. A very readable account of current scientific thinking on virtually everything discussed in this book.

Dott, Robert, and Roger L. Batten. 1981. *Evolution of the Earth*. Third edition. McGraw-Hill. A college text, this book is an excellent introduction to earth history and the major features of the fossil record.

Edwards, Fred, editor. 1980–. *Creation/Evolution*. This journal, dedicated to the promotion of evolutionary science, is the major outlet for critical examinations of creationism by scientists and educators. It is also an indispensable source of information on creationist political activities. Subscriptions, for $8.00/year, can be obtained by writing the editor at: Creation/Evolution, P.O. Box 5, Amherst Branch, Buffalo, New York 14226.

Eldredge, Niles, and Ian Tattersall. 1982. *The Myths of Human Evolution*. Columbia University Press. The "myths" include the traditional gradualistic interpretation of human evolution, and the prevailing tendency to explain cultural evolution in biological terms. The book summarizes current evolutionary theory and its controversies in more detail than presented here, and reviews the details of human biological evolution.

Futuyma, Douglas J. 1979. *Evolutionary Biology*. Sinauer Associates. An excellent college-level text on evolutionary theory by the current editor of *Evolution,* the official publication of the Society for the Study of Evolution.

Gould, Stephen Jay. 1980. *The Panda's Thumb*. W. W. Norton. The sequel to *Ever Since Darwin* (also W. W. Norton, 1977); both are collections culled from the author's monthly columns in *Natural History* magazine. The essays provide deep insight into the nature of evolutionary thought.

Johanson, Donald. 1981. *Lucy*. Simon and Schuster. The best-selling "inside story" of a young and famous hunter of human fossils. Creationists are more concerned with human evolution than with any other scientific subject (despite their denials), and it is precisely here that they are most vulnerable.

Leakey, Richard. 1977. *Making of Mankind*. E. P. Dutton. Another readable account, well illustrated, of the quest for human fossils—with emphasis, of course, on the doings of Richard and his famous family.

Sagan, Carl. 1980. *Cosmos*. Random House. An excellent review of most of the topics covered here—all in a book that, as the saying goes, needs no further introduction.

Stanley, Steven M. 1981. *The New Evolutionary Timetable*. Basic Books. A distillation of the author's technical work, *Macroevolution* (1979), this book provides a history of evolutionary thought and a spirited defense of "punctuationalism"—one side of one of evolutionary biology's current controversies. Includes a brief chapter on creationism.

John Irving

John Irving is the author whose novels
have touched the hearts and minds of
millions of readers of every age.

When Pocket Books published **THE
WORLD ACCORDING TO GARP,** it
captured the imagination of millions and
became a phenomenal bestseller.
His newest novel, **THE HOTEL NEW
HAMPSHIRE,** became an instant and
enormous bestseller in hardcover.
The reviewers across the nation have
heaped acclaim upon **THE HOTEL NEW
HAMPSHIRE,** and Irving himself has
been the subject of features in all the
media—including the cover story of <u>Time</u>.

The Writer Of Our Time— For Our Time!

John Irving has clearly become the writer of our time—for our time!

In 1982, Pocket Books will proudly publish **THE HOTEL NEW HAMPSHIRE** in paperback.

In the meantime, you can still catch up with the storytelling genius of a great writer in these John Irving novels you may have missed.

☐ **THE WORLD ACCORDING TO GARP**
(43996-0/$3.95)

☐ **SETTING FREE THE BEARS**
(44001-2/$3.50)

☐ **THE WATER-METHOD MAN**
(44002-0/$3.50)

☐ **THE 158-POUND MARRIAGE**
(44000-4/$2.95)

INFORMATION IS POWER